Health economics for non-economists

Health economics for non-economists

*An introduction to the concepts,
methods and pitfalls
of health economic evaluations*

Lieven Annemans

ACADEMIA
PRESS

© Lieven Annemans
© Academia Press
Eekhout 2
9000 Gent
Tel. +32(0)9 233 80 88   Fax +32(0)9 233 14 09
Info@academiapress.be   www.academiapress.be

Distribution:

J. Story-Scientia Scientific Booksellers
Sint-Kwintensberg 87
9000 Gent
Info@story.be   www.story.be

Annemans, Lieven
Health economics for non-economists
An introduction to the concepts, methods and pitfalls of health economic evaluations
Gent, Academia Press, 2008, XIV + 106p.

ISBN 978 90 382 1274 6
D/2008/4804/116
U 1135

All rights reserved. No part of this book may be reproduced in any form by any electronic or mechanical means (including photocopying, recording, or information storage and retrieval) without permission in writing from the publisher or the author.

Table of Contents

	Foreword	VII
	Introduction	IX
1	The purpose of health economic evaluations	1
1.1	*The goal of health care*	1
1.2	*The search for efficiency*	2
1.3	*Encouraging efficiency*	5
2	Definitions and Principles	7
2.1	*Foreword*	7
2.2	*Some definitions*	7
2.3	*Cost-effectiveness*	15
2.4	*Expressing health benefits*	18
	2.4.1 The 'unit' of health effects	18
	2.4.2 The concept of the QALY	19
	2.4.3 How should the index be measured?	21
2.5	*The limits of affordability*	25
3	Methods for economic evaluations	29
3.1	*Prospective and retrospective evaluations*	29
	3.1.1 Prospective health economic evaluations	29
	3.1.2 Retrospective health economic evaluations	33
3.2	*The decision model: general calculation principles*	34
3.3	*A real example: the prevention of deep vein thrombosis (DVT)*	42
	3.3.1 Introduction	42
	3.3.2 The DVT decision tree	42
	3.3.3 Probabilities	45
	3.3.4 Costs and QALYs	46
	3.3.5 Calculating the decision tree	48
3.4	*The Markov model*	54
3.5	*A real example of a Markov model: the treatment of breast cancer*	57
3.6	*The validity of health economic models*	67
3.7	*Sensitivity analysis*	68
3.8	*Some examples of published health economic evaluations*	76

4	Guidelines for conducting and assessing health economic evaluations		81
	4.1	*Summary of the most important guidelines*	82
		4.1.1 The medical problem and the target population	82
		4.1.2 Comparative therapies	83
		4.1.3 The perspective of the evaluation	83
		4.1.4 Design of the study	84
		4.1.5 Calculating costs	84
		4.1.6 Calculating health effects	85
		4.1.7 Time horizon	85
		4.1.8 Uncertainty analysis	86
		4.1.9 Discounting future amounts	87
		4.1.10 Conclusions and extrapolations	88
	4.2	*Specific guidelines for specific methods*	89
		4.2.1 Guidelines for models	90
		4.2.2 Guidelines for retrospective studies	92
		4.2.3 Guidelines for prospective studies	93
5	Problems with the interpretation and implementation of health economic evaluations and final considerations		95
	5.1	*When a QALY is not a QALY*	96
	5.2	*The impact on the budget*	97
	5.3	*The need for re-evaluation*	103
	5.4	*Final considerations*	104

Foreword

In recent years I have had many opportunities to explain the principles, methods, and applications of the economic evaluation of health and health care programmes to an audience of non-economists. This has been in the form of lessons for students of medicine, pharmacy or medical social sciences, and particularly with lectures for care providers such as doctors, pharmacists, nurses and physiotherapists. In the course of these activities, I have often been asked whether a practical manual, not too detailed and specifically addressed to non-economists, is available. On each occasion, I had to explain there was no such work. That is the reason for this book. It is intended for doctors, pharmacists, nurses, physiotherapists, and other health workers. It will also be useful for students of medicine, pharmacy, and health services administration. Its main aim is to outline clearly the principles and methods of health economic evaluation. After showing why we need such evaluations, it explains in detail the principles and methods which are nowadays applied in this discipline, illustrating all of them with examples from published health economic evaluations. After reading this book the reader should be able to understand these publications and – should s/he wish to – be able to participate in future studies of this nature. An additional aim is to equip the reader with the tools to confront results of such analyses: how to distinguish 'good' from 'bad' health economic evaluations, how to identify the possible pitfalls, how to interpret results and how to translate the lessons learnt into everyday medical or paramedical practice.

I would like to express my gratitude to Dr. Wim Delva, Prof. Patrick Haentjens, Prof. Hugo Robays, Dr. Rémi Brouard and Prof. Jaime Caro for their close reading of earlier versions of the manuscript which has become this book and for their highly relevant comments and suggested improvements. As indicated, the contents of this book are largely a reflection of my lectures. These usually took place in the evenings. The book itself was mainly written during weekends. For both these reasons, I would most especially like to thank my dear wife Christel and my darling children Silke, Mayke, Toon and Daan, for having the patience to put up with such frequent absences.

1) Health economic models are presented to payer to present value of money.

2) Better health care doesn't mean cheaper health care but it should not be at any cost. Cannot afford expensive treatments if they only result in minor additional effect on health.

3) Good clinical data is important to perform a good health economic evaluation.

4) Some methods include prospective and retrospective evaluations. Some limitations include lack of complete data in retrospective and sometimes artificial study protocol in prospective studies.

5) There are techniques on how good quality data is collected.

6) There is a difference between economic science and health economics.

Introduction

The economic evaluation of health and health care programmes is a discipline which has received increasing interest in recent years. In many countries, providers of new medicines or medical equipment and resources are obliged to present this sort of evaluation to give payers and/or governments a better insight into their *costs and benefits*. When a new medicine or new technology appears, the payer wants to know whether it gives *value for money*. In many western economies this payer is a health insurer or a national health system (such as the NHS in the United Kingdom). Value for money means that the money which the payer invests in this treatment is well spent. Indeed, one can only spend money once and therefore it is best to spend it as well and as wisely as possible.

But what does it mean to spend money well or spend it badly? Before we can answer this question we first have to ask ourselves why we need these so-called health economic evaluations. Chapter 1 presents arguments showing why economic evaluation of health care is important and why it can contribute to better decisions in health care and therefore also to better health care. It should be clearly stated at this point that 'better health care' does not necessarily mean cheaper health care. After all, the aim of a good health care policy is not primarily to make savings but to 'produce' health by avoiding or curing disease, so that people live longer and more healthily. As Jacobzone puts it[1]: "While the stakeholders are mostly focused on the financial relationships, the ultimate social goal of health care can be seen as producing health, which is the key factor contributing to improved well being". The ultimate aim is to achieve health gains. After all, a population in better health is more productive and will also consume more, thereby contributing to welfare.

However, this aim cannot be pursued at any cost. It is increasingly understood and accepted that "as a society we can no longer afford to pay for an expensive treatment if this treatment has only a minor additional effect on health". But what we must do is ensure that the available resources are used as well as possible and that the money

---

[1] Jacobzone S. Introduction to the Ageing-Related Diseases Project. In A Disease-based Comparison of Health Systems What is best at what cost? OECD, 2003.

allocated to health care produces as much health as possible. In fact the same principle applies in every sector where something is produced: the goal is to achieve the largest possible output (at good quality) with the available resources or to achieve a particular output with as few resources as possible (hence, savings can be useful if they can be achieved without a 'loss of health').

International organizations such as the OECD (Organisation for Economic Cooperation and Development) also emphasize that a good health policy must not only aim to be *efficient* (i.e., spend the available means as well as possible), inter alia by carrying out more economic evaluations of health care, but should also guarantee *equity* (i.e., everyone who has the same health needs should be able to obtain the same care). [2]

The health economic way of thinking and the aim for efficiency are obviously more explicit in situations where budgets for health care are more limited. If there were *no* limitation on the budget, it is more likely that *all* the new and existing preventative and curative therapies which produce a health gain would be used extensively, perhaps even if their additional effect on health was rather small. However, all budgets are limited to at least some extent and even if they increase, this growth has limits.

Therefore it is a challenge for policy to balance what is possible and what is not, within the available budget. It is just as essential that those who have an interest in participating in decision-making at least understand the principles and methods applied in the optimal allocation of resources.

Chapter 1 examines in more detail this increasing importance of economic evaluations of health care when taking decisions in health care.

Chapters 2-3 are the 'meat' of the book. The technique which is used to examine the costs and effects of interventions is known as a *health economic evaluation*. This technique combines common methods from different scientific disciplines: medicine, pharmacology, epidemiology, statistics, psychology and economics. It is important to note that

---

[2] Hurst J. In: Measuring up. Improving Health System perfomance in OECD countries. OECD 2002.

without good clinical data it is rather problematical to perform a good health economic evaluation, as we will see further. When medicines are involved in a health economic evaluation, this is often described as a pharmaco-economic evaluation. However, as indicated earlier, this sort of evaluation can concern any preventive, diagnostic or curative intervention in health care. It may also include health care programmes such as community-based preventive programmes or a pharmaceutical care programme performed by a pharmacist.

Chapter 2 attempts to explain the principles of health economic evaluations through the examination of an imaginary case study. It explains, amongst other things, the Incremental Cost-Effectiveness Ratio (ICER) and the concept of Quality Adjusted Life Years (QALY). At that point I also try to answer the question raised earlier about what is well spent money and what is not. Also included is a short but necessary intermezzo on the calculation of costs.

Chapter 3 looks at methodology in further detail. I will discuss two main methods for carrying out an economic evaluation of a particular health intervention in comparison with an alternative intervention. The first of these is through examination - either retrospectively (looking back) or prospectively (such as a randomised clinical trial) - of both the clinical data and data relating to medical consumption (how many consultations, examinations, days of hospitalisation, medicines, interventions, etc. per patient), so that in the end it is possible to measure both costs and effectiveness of the compared alternatives. This method, however, often encounters problems, the main ones being the lack of complete data in retrospective studies and the sometimes artificial study protocol in prospective studies. The more popular alternative is the application of medical decision modelling through a medical decision tree, in which the consequences of the choice of a particular intervention are examined, thereby using data from different sources. Suppose, for example, that a new medicine 'B' is compared to an existing medicine 'A' for the prevention of deep vein thrombosis (DVT). The effectiveness of B proves to be better according to the results of a clinical study: DVT occurs in 20% of patients treated with A compared to only 10% of patients treated with B. This would result in the following decision tree:

Figure 1: A simple decision tree for the prevention of DVT

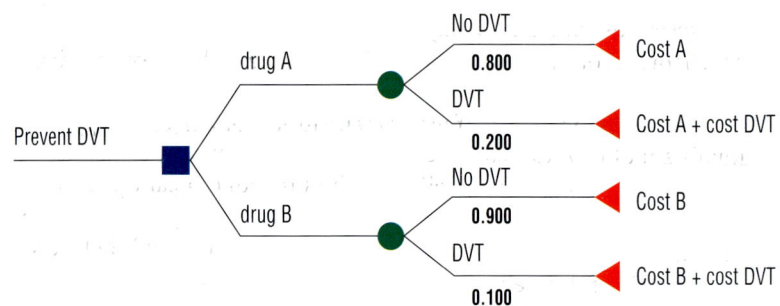

Key: the square is a *choice node* and indicates the choice between A and B. The circles are chance nodes and the triangles are value nodes.

Suppose that B is more expensive than A. It is still possible that in addition to achieving a health gain, savings can be made through the adoption of B because the chance of a DVT and thus the expense of treating it is significantly reduced. A decision tree makes it possible to examine these questions and can provide a solution to the problem. Chapter 3 discusses this technique in more detail and also looks at a more complex method, the Markov model. This is followed by an example in the field of breast cancer. This section (on decision trees and Markov models) is fairly technical. Nevertheless, it is important to struggle through because many health economic publications, often published in clinical Journals, are based on these models.

Chapter 4 describes the guidelines for carrying out good quality health economic evaluations. These evaluations usually have the aim, on the one hand, of encouraging researchers to use the best possible methods and on the other hand of permitting the users of the studies (often policymakers and care providers) to evaluate quality. There are general guidelines as well as more specific guidelines which deal, for instance, with the way in which the quality of a decision tree can be assessed or guidelines for studies in which patient data are collected retrospectively. In the discussion of these guidelines we also take a more thorough look at possible pitfalls.

The fifth and last chapter takes us back to real-life applications with an overview of the most typical problems that we come across today in the conduct and interpretation of health economic evaluations. The discipline has not stood still and a great deal of progress has been made since its introduction in policy in the late 1980s and early 1990s (with Australia and Canada in the lead). However, this does not prevent us from still being confronted with many problems. The last chapter looks at what these problems are and how we can deal with them.

I conclude with a number of recommendations for health care professionals about how to make use of this discipline, thereby also taking a look at the future. I firmly believe in the strength of health economic evaluations as a possible way to face the challenges of current health care systems, and I hope that reading this book will help the reader to share this belief.

Question:
In decision trees, where do you obtain those values? From literature? or clinical trials?

- Reasons for expenditure: ① aging population
  ② introduction of expensive treatments

- Reason why women are not screened for breast cancer at age of 40 is because: it is not efficient, costs are too high in relation to health gains.

- Three steps for evidence: ① efficacy ② effectiveness ③ efficiency.

- Health economic evaluation is only a sub-discipline of health economics.

1 The purpose of health economic evaluations

1.1 The goal of health care

In recent decades, many countries have struggled with the fact that expenditure on health care is growing much faster than the overall level of wealth (often expressed by the Gross Domestic Product, or GDP). Obviously this is a matter of concern and the question arises as to where it will end. In general, the ageing population, the introduction of expensive technologies and increasing expectations of the population with regard to better health care are given as the main reasons for the enormous growth in expenditure (we will not look at these aspects in more detail but it is worth noting that, of the above-mentioned factors, the introduction of expensive technologies is seen by most observers as the most important [3]). However, this increasing expenditure is not the only source of concern. Other problems are the great variations in the quality of care, the fact that the care provided is sometimes inadequate, non-optimal coordination between care providers, waiting times and unequal access to care. In dealing with these challenges, some policy makers and decision makers are tempted to focus in the first place on reducing health care expenses and keeping the budget under control. However, the health sector should be seen as a *productive* sector. Indeed, the aim is to produce health, by avoiding or curing disease, so that people live longer and more healthily. Furthermore, it should not be forgotten that health can be seen as an extremely important intermediate product in our economies: without health we are less productive or not productive, we engage less or not at all in leisure activities or other forms of consumerism. Without this production and consumption there is no wealth. Some might joke that the best way of making savings is to give people who are ill and giving rise to substantial costs in health care a

---

[3] Bodenheimer, 2005 Annals of Internal Medicine Volume 142, Number 10.

fatal pill so that we could save all further costs. But in fact (leaving aside for now the ethically abhorrent attitude exemplified in such a joke), recent studies have shown that on average the money invested in health care more than pays for itself.[4] Obviously, poor investments and expenditure have been made in many circumstances, while there have been very good ones in others. We should make savings wherever possible, as long as this does not stand in the way of good quality health care and therefore the production of health.

1.2 The search for efficiency

If we agree that the purpose of health care is to produce health, this is still only half of the story. Anyone who uses the word 'produce' should also mean being *productive*: health care must produce health in the most productive way and most efficient way. Why are women not screened in most countries for breast cancer from the age of forty? Why do we not vaccinate everyone against pneumococcal infections? Why is it not advisable to finance the use of cholesterol-reducing drugs for people who only have slightly raised cholesterol levels, without any other risk factors? The answer to all these questions is the same: because it is not efficient, because the costs are too high in relation to the health gains. *If we want to produce more health with the available (financial) resources, then we must allocate the money to those interventions and programmes which produce most health per invested euro or dollar or pound; that is, to the most productive and efficient ones.* As indicated earlier, money can only be spent once, and if we don't spend it wisely we miss the chance to do better things with that money.

However, as also noted above, governments and policymakers often devote more attention to making savings, without necessarily taking into account the ratio between input (money) and output (health), in other words without devoting the necessary attention to the price-quality ratio of treatments, interventions and care programmes. Annual budgets are still being presented and growth norms and savings are proposed in relation to these budgets. Nevertheless, the OECD (Organisation for Economic Cooperation and Development) clearly states that merely establishing growth norms has little or no relation with any notion of productivity or optimality. They must be

---

[4] Luce BR, Mauskopf J, Sloan FA, Ostermann J, Paramore LC. The return on investment in health care: from 1980 to 2000. Value Health. 2006 May-Jun;9(3):146-56.

replaced by measures based on health economic evaluations and by incentives to encourage efficient care.[5]

Hence, we must aim for **efficiency**. Efficiency is sometimes considered by health economists as the 'third step of evidence'.

The first step of evidence is *efficacy*: if it can be demonstrated that a medicine works better than a placebo, the medicine is said to work, to be efficacious. For example, if an anti-hypertensive drug ensures that the systolic or diastolic blood pressure decreases significantly more than with a placebo, it is said to be efficacious.

The second step is *effectiveness*. When it can be demonstrated in real situations (taking into account that the patient may have co-morbidities, is not always compliant with therapy, etc.) that a product produces health gains, it is said to be effective.[6] This means that if some patients are not treated correctly or do not consistently follow the therapy, or if side effects and/or interactions occur which give rise to a cessation of treatment, the average result will often deviate from the original clinical studies. However, it also means that it is necessary to look at relevant results. In the example of the anti-hypertensive drug, it should ideally be demonstrated that this product will reduce the probability of heart disease in the long term.

The step between efficacy and effectiveness can sometimes be quite large. Let us look at another example: it is relatively easy to demonstrate that certain treatments work to prevent osteoporosis by examining whether they maintain bone density.[7] But although bone density is important to predict the probability of fractures, this information on its own is not enough to give an accurate picture of the future probability of fractures with a medicine that improves bone density. In order to find out whether this therapy is really effective, a long-term study is required with endpoints which are relevant for the patient and society, in particular avoiding fractures, an increase in the quality of life, an increase in life expectancy, etc.

---

[5] Jacobzone S. Introduction to the Ageing-Related Diseases Project. In A Disease-based Comparison of Health Systems What is best at what cost? OECD, 2003.

[6] Davidson MH. Differences between clinical trial efficacy and real-world effectiveness. Am J Manag Care. 2006 Nov;12(15 Suppl):S405-11.

[7] Hailey D, Sampietro-Colom L, Marshall D, Rico R, Granados A, Asua J. The effectiveness of bone density measurement and associated treatments for prevention of fractures. An international collaborative review. Int J Technol Assess Health Care. 1998 Spring;14(2):237-54.

In conclusion, the bridge from efficacy to effectiveness relates to two aspects: the circumstances in which the measurements are made (from an 'artificial' clinical study environment to 'real life' situations), and what is measured (from intermediary variables to clinically and socially relevant endpoints).

Suppose there is good evidence about the effectiveness of an intervention. *It will only be considered to be efficient – the third step – when it can be demonstrated that the money spent on this intervention is money spent well.* In other words, if it would have been possible to achieve much greater health gains in any area of health with the same money by spending it on something else, the intervention being examined is relatively *in*efficient.[8]

The crucial outcome is the ratio between the resources (money) needed to carry out the intervention and its health effects. This is called the cost-effectiveness ratio. We explore this ratio more in detail in the next chapter.

As already indicated in the introduction, it is difficult to determine what is money well spent and what is not. Of course, a treatment which is extremely expensive and provides virtually no health gains is clearly not, while a treatment which leads to many health gains for a low price often is. But it should be noted that 'value for money' does not mean simply that the new treatment saves costs: as indicated above, a new treatment which costs more than current care but leads to a proportionately acceptable health gain can also provide value for money. Admittedly the ideal treatment is one which can both save costs and lead to health gains. Unfortunately such treatments are not very common, as we will see further.

Importantly, the story about providing value for money and about efficiency not only applies for individual products. It is also about the way products are used; that is, with which patients, according to which modalities. By way of example, a number of typical questions which policy makers could ask in health care are shown below:
- Are proton pump inhibitors cost-effective for patients with moderate reflux symptoms?
- For which women (i.e. of what age range) and with what frequency is it appropriate from the health economic point of view (i.e. is it value for money) to screen for breast cancer?

---

[8] Drummond MF, Sculpher MJ, O'Brien BJ, Stoddart GL, Torrance GW. Methods for the economic evaluation of health care programmes. 3rd ed. Oxford: Oxford University Press, 2005.

- Do anti-depressants provide value for money in monotherapy or in combination with psychotherapy?
- Do cholesterol-reducing drugs provide value for money for patients who have only a moderately-increased cholesterol level but no other risk factors?
- …

These few examples show that health economic evaluation and the search for efficiency is not only about the evaluation of medicines and technologies, but also about how we use these medicines and technologies. Hence it also about health care programmes and about health care interventions in general.

1.3 Encouraging efficiency

It is necessary not only to pursue efficiency, but also to encourage it. An optimum policy is based on the health care sector being a productive sector, producing the product 'health' (as described earlier). Hence it is a matter of ensuring that the 'production' takes place as efficiently as possible.

One possible approach to increasing efficiency is to formulate *health objectives*. Indeed, by setting an objective (for instance reducing the number of heart attacks in the population by x % over the next 10 years), and by assigning a budget to achieve that objective in an optimal way, overall efficiency may be encouraged. Today there are health objectives in various countries. Unfortunately, they are often determined on the basis of vague (or no) criteria and have no clear link with an available budget. They can only be useful if:
- there is a corresponding budget.
- they can be achieved in a cost-effective (efficient) way, in other words if the result is worth it given the necessary budget to achieve it.[9]

The principles of cost-effectiveness can also play a role in the *payment of doctors and other health professionals*. From this point of view, a health policy should focus not only on the application of these principles, but also on encouraging optimum medical and pharmaceuti-

---

[9] For more literature on health objectives, see Van Herten L. Health Targets. Navigating in Health Policy. TNO Prevention and Health. Leiden, The Netherlands, 2001

cal treatment. The two tasks can be combined by paying doctors (and other health professionals such as pharmacists and nurses) more than their colleagues if they act in a cost-effective way.

Once again it should be emphasised that cost-effectiveness is not only concerned with medical technologies (such as medicines) in themselves, but also, indeed above all, in the way in which these technologies are used. Cholesterol reducing drugs are cost-effective means at their current cost if they are correctly used for high-risk patients, and not if they are used, for example, for patients who merely have an increased cholesterol level but do not display any other risk factors.[10]

The cost-effective use of cost-effective technologies, medicines and programmes can be encouraged by:
- applying public funding for those technologies/medicines/programmes in their most cost-effective applications;
- limiting the financial or other obstacles to the patient's use of those cost-effective applications (e.g. by keeping the patient contribution low);
- discouraging the use of less cost-effective interventions;
- encouraging the prescriber to use this technology/medicine/programme in a cost-effective way (e.g. by paying him/her better if he/she prescribes it in a cost-effective way), a matter related to 'pay for performance'.[11]

As a final note in this introduction, it is important to understand that the 'value for money' approach is not only applicable to the health care sector, but also in other areas, such as investments in traffic safety and environmental protection. This approach could even make it possible to examine whether limited resources are better spent on health care rather than, for example, on building roundabouts at crossroads.

Hopefully the above has shown that health economic evaluations can play a key role in the provision of effective, efficient, and accessible health care. The following chapters discuss the technique of health economic evaluation in detail.

---

[10] Johannesson M. At what coronary risk level is it cost-effective to initiate cholesterol lowering drug treatment in primary prevention? European Heart Journal (2001) 22, 919–925.

[11] See for instance Rosenthal M et al. Early Experience With Pay-for-Performance. From Concept to Practice JAMA. 2005;294:1788-1793

2 Definitions and Principles

2.1 Foreword

The definitions, basic principles and methods of health economic evaluation are dealt with in this and the next chapter. The descriptions here are not entirely new. They are taken from various sources, in particular the works of David Eddy,[12] the series by Robinson in the BMJ[13] and the book of Drummond et al.,[14] supplemented by my own experiences on which ways work better than others.

2.2 Some definitions

I start by clarifying a number of terms which are often used in economic evaluations but which are sometimes used incorrectly.

Economic science is driven by scarcity. It is based on the fact that resources are limited and that choices therefore have to be made regarding their use.

---

[12] Eddy DM. Clinical decision making: from theory to practice. Cost-effectiveness analysis. A conversation with my father. JAMA. 1992 Mar 25;267(12):1669-75.
Eddy DM. Clinical decision making: from theory to practice. Cost-effectiveness analysis. Is it up to the task? JAMA. 1992 Jun 24;267(24):3342-8.
Eddy DM. Clinical decision making: from theory to practice. Cost-effectiveness analysis. Will it be accepted? JAMA. 1992 Jul 1;268(1):132-6.
Eddy DM. Clinical decision making: from theory to practice. Applying cost-effectiveness analysis. The inside story. JAMA. 1992 Nov 11;268(18):2575-82.

[13] Robinson R. Cost-benefit analysis. BMJ. 1993 Oct 9;307(6909):924-6.
Robinson R. Cost-utility analysis. BMJ. 1993 Oct 2;307(6908):859-62.
Robinson R. Cost-effectiveness analysis. BMJ. 1993 Sep 25; 307 (6907): 793-5.
Robinson R. Costs and cost-minimisation analysis. BMJ. 1993 Sep 18;307(6906):726-8.
Robinson R. Economic evaluation and health care. What does it mean? BMJ. 1993 Sep 11;307(6905):670-3.

[14] Drummond MF, Sculpher MJ, O'Brien BJ, Stoddart GL, Torrance GW. Methods for the economic evaluation of health care programmes. 3rd ed. Oxford: Oxford University Press, 2005.

Health economics is the discipline which deals with the application of economic principles and theories to health and the health sector.

Health economic evaluation is only one part of the broad discipline of health economics, as indicated in Figure 2.

Figure 2. Health economic evaluation is a sub-discipline of health economics

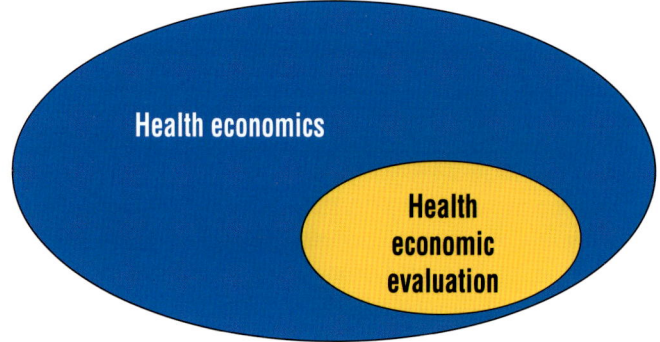

Other sub-disciplines deal with, amongst other things, the balance between supply and demand of health care, methods of financing and organizing health care and specific subjects such as the optimal size of hospitals, the optimal size of patient contributions and optimal ways of paying doctors.

This book deals mainly with health economic evaluations.

> *A health economic evaluation is defined as a comparative analysis of both the costs and the health effects of two or more alternative health interventions.*

The important elements in the definitions are, on the one hand, the *comparison* of alternatives and on the other hand, the *two dimensions* of costs and health effects.

In most cases new interventions in health care will give rise both to higher costs and also to more effectiveness in comparison with the therapies already available. An economic evaluation makes it possible to examine whether the money that would be invested in a new intervention for a particular condition would actually be used efficiently. This is done by means of comparisons with the current therapy. Note that in this context 'current therapy' may also be the 'do option.

In exceptional cases the cost of the intervention is entirely recovered by savings resulting from avoided disease, complications, or side effects.

These are known as *net saving interventions*. A number of examples of treatments leading, according to health economic studies, to net savings are shown below:

- the preventive treatment with aspirin of people with a risk of coronary disease of 1% or more per year, in comparison with no prevention;[15]
- the treatment with sartans for diabetic patients with microalbuminuria and hypertension to prevent end stage renal disease, in comparison with standard antihypertensive treatment;[16]
- diet and physical exercise for patients with glucose intolerance to prevent diabetes, in comparison with no prevention;[17]
- alendronate for patients with at least one vertebral fracture to prevent further fractures, in comparison with calcium and vitamin D only;[18]
- escitalopram compared to venlafaxine for the treatment of major depression;[19]
- sartans for the treatment of patients with heart failure who are intolerant to ACE inhibitors, in comparison with the standard treatment.[20]

---

[15] Annemans L, Lamotte et al. Which patients should receive aspirin for primary prevention of cardiovascular disease? An economic evaluation. J Clin Pract. 2006 Sep;60(9):1129-37.

[16] Palmer A et al. Cost-Effectiveness of Early Irbesartan Treatment Versus Control (Standard Antihypertensive Medications Excluding ACE Inhibitors, Other Angiotensin-2 Receptor Antagonists, and Dihydropyridine Calcium Channel Blockers) or Late Irbesartan Treatment in Patients With Type 2 Diabetes, Hypertension, and Renal Disease. Diabetes Care, Vol 27, nr 8, August 2004.

[17] Lindgren P, et al. Lifestyle intervention to prevent diabetes in men and women with impaired glucose tolerance is cost-effective. Int J Technol Assess Health Care. 2007 Spring;23(2):177-83.

[18] Strom O, et al. Cost-effectiveness of alendronate in the treatment of postmenopausal women in 9 European countries - an economic evaluation based on the fracture intervention trial. Osteoporos Int. 2007 Feb 28.

[19] Llorca PM, Fernandez JL. Escitalopram in the treatment of major depressive disorder: clinical efficacy, tolerability and cost-effectiveness vs. venlafaxine extended-release formulation. Int J Clin Pract. 2007 Apr;61(4):702-10.

[20] McMurray JJ, et al. Resource utilization and costs in the Candesartan in Heart failure: Assessment of Reduction in Mortality and morbidity (CHARM) programme. Eur Heart J. 2006 Jun;27(12):1447-58.

It should be noted that for the description of the above examples, I tried to use the so-called 'PICO' framework, which gives information about: P 'patient'; I 'intervention'; C 'comparison'; and O 'outcome'. This framework makes it clearer what we are talking about and decreases the risk of generalised conclusions.

It is possible to represent net savings graphically, as shown in Figure 3, which examines a new medicine in comparison with an existing medicine for the treatment of a particular disease. In the example here, the purchasing cost of the new medicine is considerably higher than that of the current treatment, as indicated on the left of the figure (purchasing cost). However, because the new medicine is also significantly better than the current medicine, this will result in overall savings because, for example, less follow-up is required and/or there is a smaller chance of hospitalisation. This is shown in the central part of the figure: the average patient who receives the new treatment will require lower expenditure for consultations, hospitalisations, examinations and so on.

When everything is added together and we consider the point of view of the health care payer (e.g. an insurance company, a national health service, a managed care organization), we find that the higher purchasing cost of the new treatment is more than compensated for by the savings elsewhere, so that we end up with a situation in which on average the new treatment will lead to net savings for the payer.

Figure 3: Illustration of a net saving technology compared with the current treatment

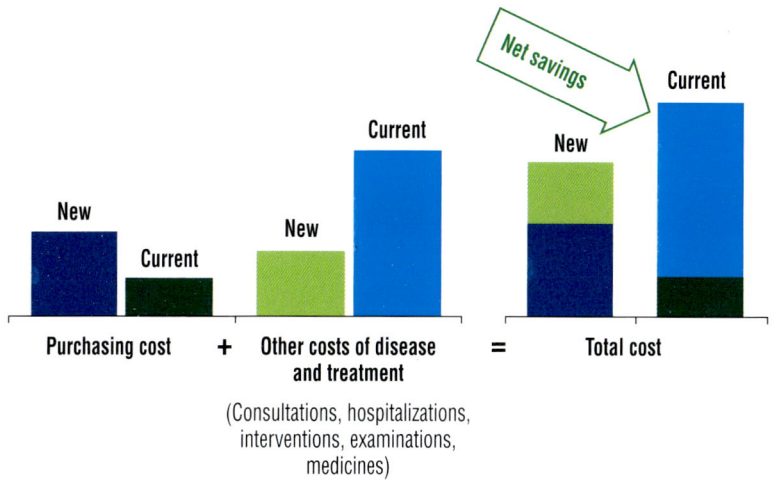

The example in Figure 3 is fairly exceptional, however. In most cases there will still be net costs related to a new technology or treatment in health care. This is illustrated by Figure 4, in which the new treatment is still more expensive than the current treatment and the average patient who receives the new treatment will still cause lower costs in the other fields than if the current treatment were followed, but the differences in the middle part of the figure are now less pronounced.

Figure 4: Illustration of a new technology which causes net costs

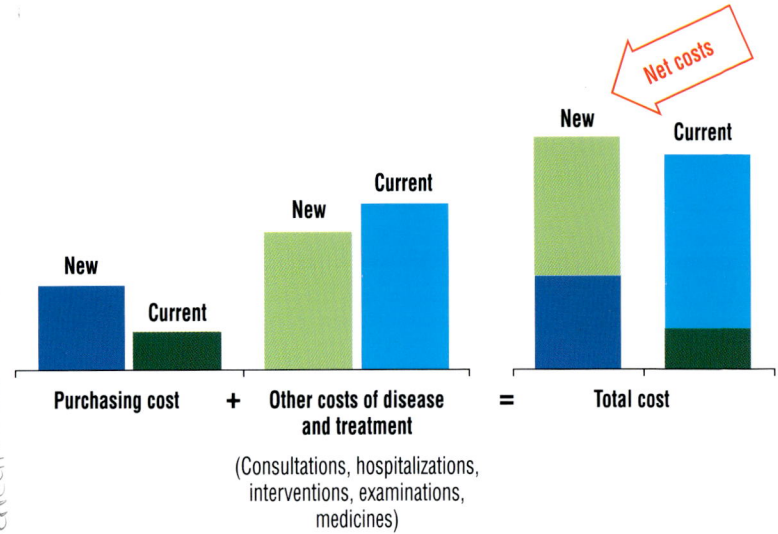

The result is that the total costs of treating a patient with the new therapy are higher than with the current therapy, as shown on the right of the figure. In these cases the definition of a health economic evaluation becomes apparent: we need to look at the two dimensions, costs and effects. Thus we have to balance the net costs in relation to the net health effects. That is why a health economic evaluation is often known as a *cost-effectiveness analysis*.

It should be noted that the new treatment can even be more expensive than the current treatment with regard to the other costs as well. Suppose, for example, that for patients with metastatic cancer, life can be extended by six months. In that case the patient will cause extra costs during those six months for hospitalisation, examinations, consultations, and so on. The new treatment will then not only lead to extra purchasing costs but also to extra costs in other areas. However, as the definition shows, and as we know by now, both dimensions - the costs and the health effects - must be examined.

2 Definitions and Principles

Intermezzo on costs

Before we go deeper into cost-effectiveness analysis, it should be noted that most analyses are limited to what are called *direct medical costs*. These are health care costs which are paid by the government, health insurance and/or the patient.

It is possible, however, to take additional costs into account, in particular, *direct non-medical costs* (for example, travel costs, or time spent by family members providing care) as well as the *indirect non-medical costs*, which are basically the costs resulting from loss of productivity (for example, the average patient receiving the current therapy might be off work longer than the patient on the new therapy).[21]

There are also the *indirect medical costs*. These relate to the general costs of health care (not only the costs related to the disease being examined) which can arise in the future. For example, if a patient lives longer as a result of a new intervention to prevent myocardial infarctions, the future costs linked to this longer life - for example if the patient later develops Parkinson's or Alzheimer's - can also be taken into account. Obviously, such expected costs are calculated on the basis of statistics on the average cost of health care per age category. However, these indirect medical costs (although they can be very high) are rarely included in calculations. It would, of course, be ethically/socially intolerable not to carry out medical interventions on the grounds that people will have more medical needs by living longer.[22] For an example of including this type of costs, see, amongst others, Lamotte et al.[23]

---

[21] Koopmanschap, M., Rutten, F. A practical guide for calculating indirect costs of disease. PharmacoEconomics 1996; 10 (5): 460-466.

[22] Johannesson M, Meltzer D, O'Conor RM. Incorporating future costs in medical cost-effectiveness analysis: implications for the cost-effectiveness of the treatment of hypertension. Med Decis Making. 1997;17(4):382-9.

[23] Lamotte M et al. A Multi-Country Health Economic Evaluation of Highly Concentrated N-3 Polyunsaturated Fatty Acids in Secondary Prevention after Myocardial Infarction. Pharmacoeconomics 2006; 24 (8): 783-795.

In conclusion, the following types of costs can be distinguished:

	Direct	**Indirect**
Medical	Costs related to the disease from the perspective of the health care payer(s)	Future health care costs
Non-medical	Costs which do not arise in the health sector, but which are related to the disease, e.g., travelling expenses, special diet	Loss of productivity as a result of absenteeism or early death

The decision about the type of costs to be included in a health economic evaluation depends on the *perspective* of that evaluation. If the perspective of the health care payer is taken, then direct medical costs are included. When a new treatment avoids heart attacks, and a health economic evaluation is performed whereby the savings due to avoided heart attacks are to be calculated, then only the cost of heart attacks from the payer's perspective will be taken into account. If, however, a broader societal perspective is taken, then the productivity losses due to a heart attack are also taken into account.

The hospital perspective

In some health economic evaluations a more narrow perspective is chosen, namely the perspective of the hospital manager. Here, the purpose is to calculate the costs and savings from the perspective of the hospital manager. If, for example, a new treatment for postoperative pain is introduced, with less time consumption for nurses and physicians, this treatment results in potential savings from the hospital manager's perspective.

Here as well, different types of costs can be identified:

Fixed costs versus variable costs: Fixed costs remain the same, no matter how much health care is provided. For instance, the cost of a pain pump is a fixed cost, because whether there are 20 patients treated per year with this pump or 100, its cost remains the same. A variable cost increases with the amount of delivered care. Drugs represent a typical example of variable cost.

Direct versus indirect costs: direct costs are immediately related to a disease or condition. For instance, a pain pump represents a direct cost, because it is directly linked to the treatment of pain. Indirect costs (in this classification) are those *not* related to a given disease. For instance a CT scanner represents an indirect cost, because it can be applied for various types of indications.

Note, therefore, that in the literature the term 'indirect cost' is used for three different concepts: first when referring to the type of cost as just described above (with the example of the CT scanner), second when referring to productivity related costs, as in 'indirect non medical costs' and third when referring to future medical costs, defined as 'indirect medical costs'. So, when you see the term 'indirect costs' appearing, make sure you understand what exactly is meant.

2.3 Cost-effectiveness

We have now arrived at the concept of cost-effectiveness. The basic principles of a cost-effectiveness analysis are relatively simple. The approach consists of three steps:

1) The calculation of the difference in total costs between New and Current (C_N-C_C). This is shown in Figure 3 and Figure 4 above. It should be noted that this difference is one of net cost; that is, it takes any savings into account.

2) The calculation of the difference in effectiveness between New and Current (E_N-E_C). If the new treatment is more effective it will result in a *net health gain*. Note that, just as costs are expressed in euros or pounds and body weight expressed in kilos or pounds, we can express this health gain in units. A frequently applied unit of health, the QALY, is dealt with in Section 2.4.

3) The calculation of the *Incremental Cost-Effectiveness Ratio* (**ICER**) (C_N-C_C)/(E_N-E_C).

It should be noted that, despite the terms commonly used in this formula, a comparison does not necessarily involve a 'new' and a 'current' treatment. It is perfectly possible to make such comparisons between two existing treatments. However, in the rest of this exposition I will mostly work with 'new' in comparison with 'current', because this is the most common situation.

Results can be graphically expressed in two dimensions. Usually the representation that is used is that shown in Figure 5. In that figure, the current treatment is shown in the origin. The new treatment or intervention is then shown in relation to the difference in the effect (represented on the X axis) and the difference in cost (represented on the Y axis) in relation to the current treatment.

Figure 5: Illustration of a new treatment compared to the current treatment in two dimensions

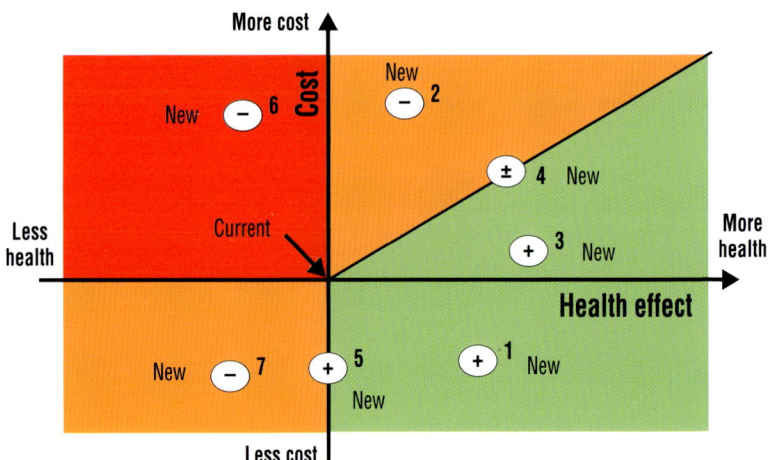

It is possible that the new treatment is cheaper and more effective than the current treatment (situation 1). In that case the new treatment appears below and to the right of the current treatment and is known as the *dominant* treatment. However, if the new treatment is more expensive than the current treatment and does not lead to significant health gains (situation 2), most policy makers will decide that this treatment is not worth the money and is therefore not efficient, not *cost-effective*.

On the other hand, in situation 3 there are admittedly extra costs, but there is an important health gain as well. In that case the new treatment is considered to be cost-effective.

Where is the threshold? In other words, if situation 2 is not cost-effective while situation 3 *is* cost-effective, there must be a threshold somewhere, above which the new treatment is not deemed cost-effective. The question we must ask, therefore, is how much money the health care payer is willing to pay to gain 'one unit' of health. In order to answer this question we must determine what 'one unit' of health is. This is done in the following section. What we can already state with some certainty here is that if there were enough money, the payer would possibly pay for everything that is shown on the right side of the current treatment, and therefore also for Situation 2. But if there is not enough money, this threshold of *maximum willingness to pay for a unit of health* must be established. This threshold is illustrated by the diagonal line and situation 4, which falls exactly on that line.

Finally, there are a few special cases. In situation 5 the new treatment is just as good as the present treatment, but cheaper. In that case there should be no discussion: the new treatment is dominant.

In conclusion, situations 1, 3, 4, and 5 are cost-effective. Furthermore, situations 1 and 5 are dominant.

In situation 6 the new treatment is less effective and more expensive. In that case the new treatment is *dominated* by the current treatment and does not deserve use. In situation 7 the new treatment is cheaper, but less good. If this new treatment were to be used, savings would be made but there would also be a loss of health. The question in this case is how much health policymakers are prepared to lose. The answer to this question is less clear. That is why I do not draw a threshold in the bottom left quadrant.

2.4 Expressing health benefits

2.4.1 The 'unit' of health effects

In order to be able to express the threshold of maximum social willingness to pay, we must find a unit, as indicated above, to express health gains. In health economic evaluations we find several indicators of health gain:
- Number of cured patients
- Number of complications avoided
- Number of symptom-free days
- Number of days without symptoms or toxicity
- Number of days of good quality of life
- Number of years without complications
- Number of years in a 'responder' state
- Number of life years
- Disability adjusted life years (DALY) (life years adjusted by a disability level)
- Quality adjusted life years (QALY) (life years adjusted by a quality level)

Consider for instance the number of symptom-free days: if a medicine results in 10 extra days without symptoms in a period of one year and it costs €300 more than the current treatment per year (net cost), the incremental cost-effectiveness ratio on this particular parameter is €300/10 = €30 per symptom-free day.

The question then becomes: is that a good or a bad result? To answer this question we need a reference point: what is generally considered as an acceptable cost for gaining one symptom-free day? There is no general answer to this question because a day with symptoms of, for example, oesophagitis is not comparable to a day of neuropathic pain or asthma. Yet such an approach can be taken if one is to make a decision *within* one specific disease area. Suppose it has been decided to make the reduction of smokers a major health objective, and a budget has been assigned for this purpose. In this case, expressing the cost-effectiveness of alternative anti-tobacco interventions in terms of "how many extra Euros (or Pounds or Dollars) are required to avoid one smoker?" would be an adequate approach in selecting the most cost-effective intervention.

On the other hand, if one wants to make comparisons between different interventions *across* different diseases ("is a new chemotherapy in the treatment of colorectal cancer more cost-effective than a new antihypertensive in the prevention of heart disease?"), then only the last two in the list above, namely the DALY and the QALY, seem to be suitable. The QALY is explained in detail in the next section, at the end of which the DALY is compared to it.

2.4.2 The concept of the QALY

QALY stands for *Quality Adjusted Life Years*. The principle of the QALY is that the quality and quantity of life can be combined in one concept. This is illustrated in Figure 6 (A, B, C, D). The Y axis in every case shows an index between 0 and 1, where 1 is equal to full health and 0 stands for no health. The index expresses the *utility* level, which can be considered – in simple terms – as a 'quality of life' level.

Imagine now that a patient with a particular disease has lived for 10 years from the time of the diagnosis. Suppose that the average 'quality of life' during these 10 years had a value of 0.6 on this scale between 0 and 1. It is then said that this patient has had 0.6 x 10 = 6 QALYs. Each of the 10 years of life is assigned a 'weight' of 0.6, and the number of life years is adjusted to the quality of those life years, hence the term 'quality adjusted life years'. Thus the QALY is the result of multiplying the quantity and the quality of life. A patient who lived for 6 years in perfect health would also have 6 QALYs (6 years times 1).

If it had been possible for the patient to live 2 years longer with a therapy to extend his life, but the quality of life expressed by the index does not change, the health gain would be 0.6 x 2 = 1.2 QALYs (Figure 6B). The gain in QALYs is equal to the difference between the surfaces under the two curves (7.2 -6 = 1.2).

If it had been possible to improve the quality of the patient's life to 0.7, and do so for a period of 10 years, a gain of health would have been achieved equal to (0.7-0.6) x 10 = 0.1 x 10 = 1QALY (Figure 6C). Hence, it is also possible for someone to gain QALYs without increasing his/her life expectancy! For example, the use of so-called 'biologicals' in Crohn's disease, rheumatoid arthritis and psoriasis usually improves patients' quality of life while not increasing their life expectancy.

Obviously, if an effect is achieved both with regard to the quality and the quantity of life, more QALYs are gained. If the patient had lived for 12 years with a quality of 0.7, the total number of QALYs would be 0.7 x 12 = 8.4, 2.4 more QALYs than in the starting situation (Figure 6D). For instance, most treatments in primary cancer will increase both quality of life and life expectancy. Another example: Cardiac Resynchronisation Therapy reduces all-cause mortality rates and improves quality of life in patients with chronic heart failure. [24]

Figure 6: Graphical representation of the QALY

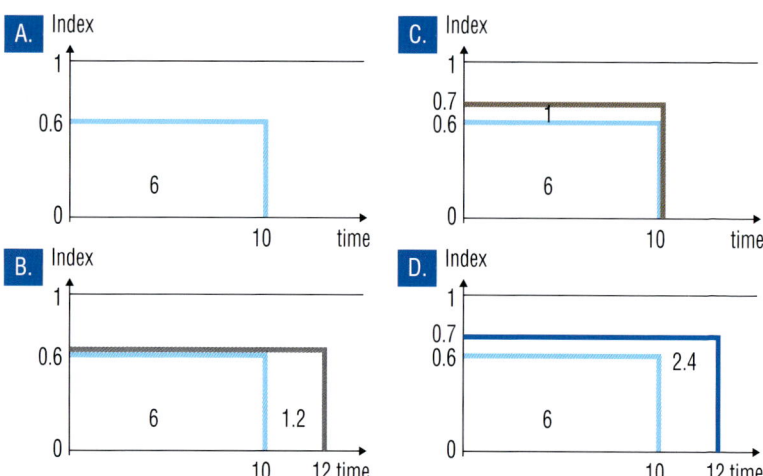

In reality, of course, the level of the index between 0 and 1 is not constant. Torrance pointed this out in one of the very first publications on the topic. A more realistic representation of the average evolution of a patient is given in Figure 7. [25] Once again the gain in QALYs is equal to the difference between the surfaces below the two curves. Note the loss of QALYs at the beginning of the treatment in this example (the result of side effects). Note also that in order for a graph like Figure 7 to be produced, many time points for observation are required, which in practice are rarely available.

---

[24] Fox M et al. The clinical effectiveness and cost-effectiveness of cardial resynchronisation (biventricular pacing) for heart failure: systematic review and economic model. Health Technol Assess. 2007; 11(47): iii-iv, ix-248.

[25] Based on Torrance G. Utility approach for measuring health-related quality of life. J Chron Dis. 1987, Vol. 40, No 6: 593-600

Figure 7: Graphical representation of the QALY (2)

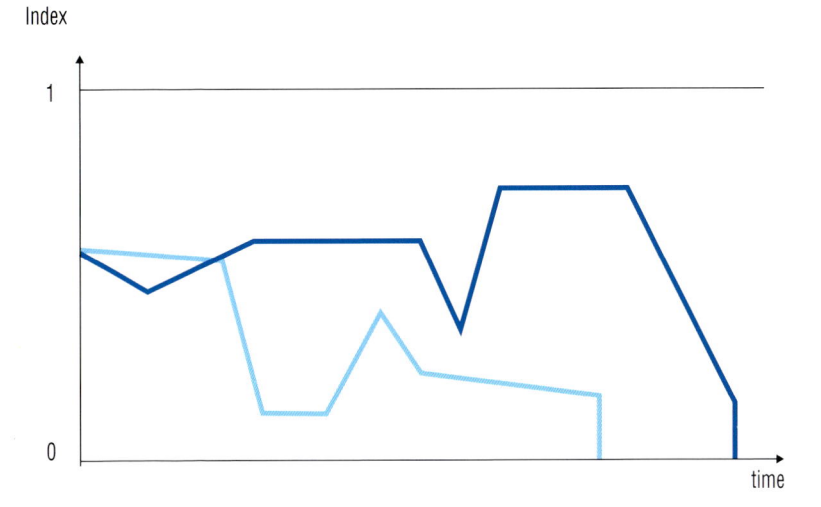

Key: Dark blue curve = new intervention; light blue curve = current treatment

2.4.3 How should the index be measured?

The value between 0 and 1, the index, is a kind of measurement of the quality of life of a person at a particular moment. In fact, the index is not related so much to the health state itself, but *to the way in which that state of health is perceived*. This is why, as noted above, the term *utility* is also used. The term is borrowed from the economic theory which states that the choice of a person between two or more products is determined by his budget, the price of those products and *the utility he gains in his choice*. If someone chooses ('prefers') chocolate rather than bread (assuming the two cost the same) this is because that person derives more utility from consuming chocolate. The same applies for health and sickness: the index, the utility, expresses to what extent a person has a *preference* for a particular state of health. This preference is expressed between 0 and 1.

There are various methods to measure this utility level. The most commonly used method today is the method based on generic quality of life questionnaires such as the SF-36 or the EuroQol 5D (EQ-5D). The latter questionnaire contains five questions, each with three possible answers. A profile is drawn up on the basis of these answers.

Figure 8 shows these five questions.

In principle the EQ-5D questionnaire is also accompanied by a scale in which '100' is the best possible health state one can imagine and '0' the worst. However, the utility level is calculated on the basis of the answers to the five questions. Since each question has 3 possible answers, there are altogether $3 \times 3 \times 3 \times 3 \times 3 = 3^5 = 243$ possible profiles.

Figure 8: The five main questions in the EQ-5D questionnaire[26]

Mobility
1. I have no problems in walking about ❏
2. I have some problems in walking about ❏
3. I am confined to bed ❏

Self-Care
1. I have no problems with self-care ❏
2. I have some problems washing or dressing myself ❏
3. I am unable to wash or dress myself ❏

Usual Activities (e.g. work, study, housework, family or leisure activities)
1. I have no problems with performing my usual activities ❏
2. I have some problems with performing my usual activities ❏
3. I am unable to perform my usual activities ❏

Pain/Discomfort
1. I have no pain or discomfort ❏
2. I have moderate pain or discomfort ❏
3. I have extreme pain or discomfort ❏

Anxiety/Depression
1. I am not anxious or depressed ❏
2. I am moderately anxious or depressed ❏
3. I am extremely anxious or depressed ❏

---

[26] Cleemput I. et al. Measuring health state preferences in Belgium with the EQ-5D: a pilot survey in health care workers. Arch Public Health 2003, 61, 201-214

An example of a profile may for instance be: 12222
I have no problems in walking about	*1*
I have some problems washing or dressing myself	*2*
I have some problems with performing my usual activities	*2*
I have moderate pain or discomfort	*2*
I am moderately anxious or depressed	*2*

Such a profile is then translated into a 'utility' score. The determination of the score for any one person/patient has been arrived at by the development of mathematical algorithms based on health-state valuation studies in the general population. For anyone who wants to know more about this, reference may be made to Drummond et al.[14]

The important point is that in this way it has been possible to determine a utility for every profile, and to do so in different countries. For instance, the scoring that is applied in Belgium is shown in Figure 9. More information can be found on http://www.euroqol.org/

Another 'popular' quality of life instrument that also allows patient profiles to be translated into utility values is the short form 36 (SF36), consisting of 36 questions, each with 5 possible answers (see http://www.sf-36.org/).

It should be noted that negative values appear in Figure 9. For instance, a person who is in a condition 33333, has a utility value of -0.1584. Hence, according to this concept, a condition in which someone is confined to bed, unable to wash or dress himself, unable to perform usual activities, has extreme pain or discomfort and is extremely anxious or depressed, is worse than death.

It should also be noted that when health effects are expressed in QALYs, some health economists apply the term incremental cost *utility* ratio (ICUR). Others simply state that the QALY is a parameter of effectiveness and prefer the term incremental cost-effectiveness ratio (ICER). The approach taken in this book is the latter.

Figure 9: Utility levels corresponding to EuroQol 5D profiles [27]

status	index	status	index	status	index	status	index	status	index
11111	1.0000	12322	0.2602	21233	0.1121	23231	0.1536	32133	-0.0142
11112	0.7444	12323	0.1568	21311	0.4555	23232	0.0502	32211	0.3291
11113	0.3847	12331	0.2799	21312	0.3521	23233	-0.0532	32212	0.2257
11121	0.7641	12332	0.1765	21313	0.2487	23311	0.2902	32213	0.1223
11122	0.6607	12333	0.0731	21321	0.3718	23312	0.1868	32221	0.2455
11123	0.3010	13111	0.4262	21322	0.2684	23313	0.0834	32222	0.1421
11131	0.4241	13112	0.3228	21323	0.1650	23321	0.2065	32223	0.0387
11132	0.3207	13113	0.2194	21331	0.2881	23322	0.1031	32231	0.1618
11133	0.2173	13121	0.3425	21332	0.1847	23323	-0.0003	32232	0.0584
11211	0.8170	13122	0.2391	21333	0.0813	23331	0.1228	32233	-0.0450
11212	0.7136	13123	0.1357	22111	0.6907	23332	0.0194	32311	0.2984
11213	0.3539	13131	0.2588	22112	0.5873	23333	-0.0840	32312	0.1950
11221	0.7333	13132	0.1554	22113	0.2276	31111	0.4426	32313	0.0916
11222	0.6299	13133	0.0520	22121	0.6070	31112	0.3392	32321	0.2147
11223	0.2702	13211	0.3954	22122	0.5036	31113	0.2358	32322	0.1113
11231	0.3934	13212	0.2920	22123	0.1439	31121	0.3589	32323	0.0079
11232	0.2900	13213	0.1886	22131	0.2670	31122	0.2555	32331	0.1310
11233	0.1866	13221	0.3117	22132	0.1636	31123	0.1521	32332	0.0276
11311	0.5300	13222	0.2083	22133	0.0602	31131	0.2752	32333	-0.0758
11312	0.4266	13223	0.1049	22211	0.6599	31132	0.1718	33111	0.2773
11313	0.3232	13231	0.2280	22212	0.5565	31133	0.0684	33112	0.1739
11321	0.4463	13232	0.1246	22213	0.1968	31211	0.4118	33113	0.0705
11322	0.3429	13233	0.0212	22221	0.5762	31212	0.3084	33121	0.1936
11323	0.2395	13311	0.3646	22222	0.4728	31213	0.2050	33122	0.0902
11331	0.3626	13312	0.2612	22223	0.1131	31221	0.3281	33123	-0.0132
11332	0.2592	13313	0.1578	22231	0.2362	31222	0.2247	33131	0.1099
11333	0.1558	13321	0.2810	22232	0.1328	31223	0.1213	33132	0.0065
12111	0.7651	13322	0.1776	22233	0.0294	31231	0.2444	33133	-0.0969
12112	0.6617	13323	0.0742	22311	0.3728	31232	0.1410	33211	0.2465
12113	0.3020	13331	0.1973	22312	0.2694	31233	0.0376	33212	0.1431
12121	0.6815	13332	0.0939	22313	0.1660	31311	0.3810	33213	0.0397
12122	0.5781	13333	-0.0095	22321	0.2892	31312	0.2776	33221	0.1628
12123	0.2184	21111	0.7733	22322	0.1858	31313	0.1742	33222	0.0594
12131	0.3415	21112	0.6699	22323	0.0824	31321	0.2974	33223	-0.0440
12132	0.2381	21113	0.3102	22331	0.2055	31322	0.1940	33231	0.0791
12133	0.1347	21121	0.6897	22332	0.1021	31323	0.0906	33232	-0.0243
12211	0.7344	21122	0.5863	22333	-0.0013	31331	0.2137	33233	-0.1277
12212	0.6310	21123	0.2266	23111	0.3517	31332	0.1103	33311	0.2157
12213	0.2713	21131	0.3497	23122	0.1646	31333	0.0069	33312	0.1123
12221	0.6507	21132	0.2463	23123	0.0612	32111	0.3599	33313	0.0089
12222	0.5473	21133	0.1429	23131	0.1844	32112	0.2565	33321	0.1320
12223	0.1876	21211	0.7426	23132	0.0810	32112	0.2565	33322	0.0286
12231	0.3108	21212	0.6392	23133	-0.0224	32113	0.1531	33323	-0.0748
12232	0.2073	21213	0.2795	23211	0.3209	32121	0.2762	33331	0.0484
12233	0.1039	21221	0.6589	23212	0.2175	32121	0.2762	33332	-0.0550
12311	0.4473	21222	0.5555	23213	0.1141	32122	0.1728	33333	-0.1584
12312	0.3439	21223	0.1958	23221	0.2373	32123	0.0694	Dead	0.0000
12313	0.2405	21231	0.3189	23222	0.1339	32131	0.1926		
12321	0.3636	21232	0.2155	23223	0.0305	32132	0.0892		

[27] www.kce.fgov.be Federal Knowledge Centre for Health Care; Report 28A.

Finally, a brief explanation of the DALY (Disability Adjusted Life Year): this concept, put forward by the WHO, combines the time that a person spends in disability and the time lost due to premature death. Thus it is very similar to the QALY. There are two important differences:

1. The weight between 0 and 1 of the condition in which the patient finds himself is now equal to 1 in the poorest possible condition and 0 in full health.

2. The weights were arrived at on the basis of a consensus of experts and are therefore not 'utilities' (in the economic sense).

One DALY represents the loss of a year in full health and is therefore a measurement of the number of healthy years of life that are lost. As an example we can take the situation of a 60-year-old person who could normally live to the age of 80 in good health.
If this person becomes ill at the age of 60 with a disability score of 0.8 and then dies at the age of 70, the number of DALYs is 0.8x10 (lived for 10 years with a disability of 0.8) + 10 (died 10 years prematurely) = 18 DALYs. For more information on the DALY and a critical assessment, reference may be made to Arnesen and Nord. [28]

2.5 The limits of affordability

The previous sections discussed the concepts of incremental cost and incremental effect, as well as the ratio between both. The higher the ratio, the worse the result. We have also seen that there is such a thing as a maximal acceptable ratio.
This brings us to the threshold of willingness to pay for health gains. Suppose a new therapy for primary breast cancer costs €30,000 (net cost). In the long term the therapy also leads to an average of 3 QALYs gained. The incremental cost-effectiveness ratio is then €30,000 / 3 = €10,000 per QALY. Another treatment which costs only €5,000 but results in only 0.1 QALY will cost €5,000/0.1 = €50,000 per QALY gained, which is a worse (less efficient) result. Note that the result is always expressed with a denominator of one QALY in order to see for what it costs to gain one QALY.

---

[28] Arnesen T, Nord E. The value of DALY life: problems with ethics and validity of disability adjusted life years. BMJ. 1999 Nov 27;319(7222):1423-5.

The next question is now: "How much money is a payer prepared to pay for a gain of one QALY in the population?" Several papers on this question have been published in a variety of countries. The findings have been summarized by Jolain (2006).[29] Table 1 presents this summary, with results expressed in Euros per QALY.

Table 1:   Summary of the published thresholds of the willingness to pay for a QALY*

Country	Currency	Threshold in local currency	Threshold in Euro
USA	USD	50000-100000	36600-73200
Sweden	SEK	500000	54000
UK	GBP	30000	44500
Australia	AUSD	42000-76000	26200-47400
Canada	CND	20000-100000	13700-68700
The Netherlands	EURO	20000	20000
New Zealand	NZD	20000	11200

* Conversion into euros based on exchange rates of 1 August 2007.

The table shows that the willingness to pay varies from country to country quite widely. The maximal willingness to pay for gaining one QALY appears to be around €20,000 in The Netherlands as compared to >€50,000 in Sweden. The time period of the publication and the author's country of origin are probably the most important factors. It is particularly striking that a number of studies/countries adopt a double limit. In these cases, the interpretation is that when the result of a health economic evaluation is lower (= better) than the lower limit, the chance of acceptance by the payer is greater, while when the result is above the upper limit, the chance of acceptance is small.

According to Rawlins and Cuyler,[30] this sort of double threshold exists in the United Kingdom. Figure 10 shows how, according to these authors, the chance of non-acceptance is small when the incremental cost-effectiveness ratio (ICER) is lower than £5,000 - £15,000 per QALY, but high when the ICER is larger than £25,000 - £35,000 per QALY. If such a curve exists, there are in fact no thresholds; rather there is an increasing probability of non acceptance with higher ICERs.

[30] Rawlins MD and Culyer AJ, National Institute for Clinical Excellence and its value judgments. BMJ 2004;329:224-227 (24 July).

In Australia, where there has been experience with health economic evaluations since the early 1990s, a similar tendency may be observed. George et al[31] found in a review of 355 reimbursement files that not a single medicine was reimbursed with an ICER > \$AU75,286 per QALY and that, on the other hand, only one medicine was not reimbursed with an ICER < \$AU19,807 per QALY. These authors quote a double limit for willingness to pay between \$AU42,000 (below which the chance of refusal is very small) and \$AU76,000 per QALY (above which the chance of acceptance is very small).

Figure 10: Double limit of societal willingness to pay for a QALY[30]

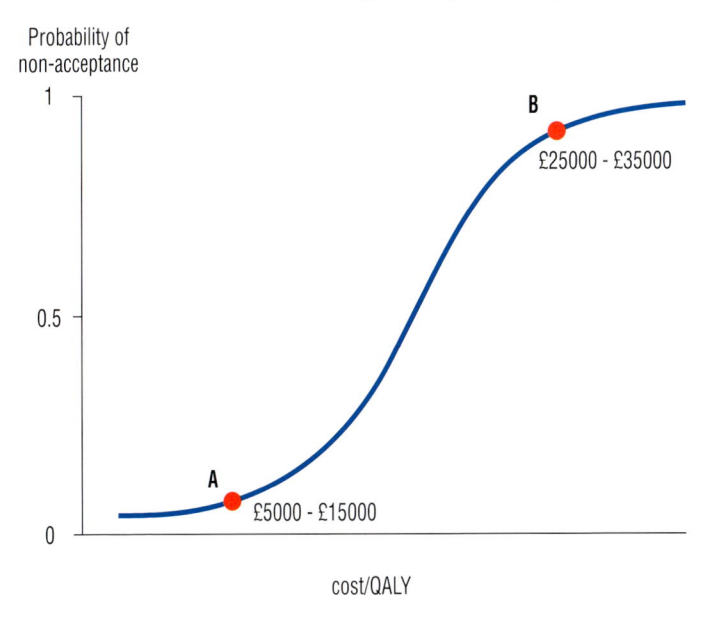

Probability of non-acceptance

- Point A: £5000 - £15000
- Point B: £25000 - £35000

cost/QALY

The World Health Organization (WHO) states that the limit for being prepared to pay should be related to the wealth of a country.[32] Following this rationale, a result expressed in cost per QALY which is lower than the level of the Gross Domestic Product per person would be called cost-effective. For example, in a country where the GDP per

---

[31] George B, Harris A, Mitchell A. Cost-effectiveness analysis and the consistency of decision making: evidence from pharmaceutical reimbursement in Australia (1991 to 1996). Pharmacoeconomics. 2001;19(11):1103-9.

[32] Macro-economics and Health; investing in health for economic development. Report of the commission on macroeconomics and health. W.C.o.M.a. Health. Editor 2001: Geneva.

inhabitant is approximately €30,000 per year, a health economic evaluation resulting in an ICER < €30,000 would indicate a cost-effective intervention.

The following chapter examines in greater detail the methods used to arrive at the ICER.

3 Methods for economic evaluations

The introduction introduced roughly two methods for carrying out an economic evaluation of health interventions:
1°. A comparative study is organised, either retrospectively (looking back), or prospectively (such as a randomised clinical study), in which not only clinical data are collected but also data relating to medical consumption (how many consultations, examinations, days of hospitalisation, medicines, interventions, etc. per patient). As a result, not only the effectiveness of the alternatives being compared is measured, but also the total cost.
2°. The technique of modelling is applied. On the basis of a decision model, the consequences of a particular choice are presented, using data from different sources. Below I first discuss retrospective and prospective evaluations, followed by the technique of decision modelling.

3.1 Prospective and retrospective evaluations

At first sight, a direct comparative study, either retrospective or prospective, of the alternative treatments to be examined appears to be the best approach. A number of patients are receiving intervention A (current), while other patients are receiving intervention B (new), and all data (clinical and economic) are recorded for the patients in both groups. Unfortunately, in practice it is not as simple as that.

3.1.1 Prospective health economic evaluations

By way of example, let us consider patients with a hip replacement. Suppose we want to find out whether prolonged medication with low molecular weight heparins (LMWH) after the patient is discharged is cost-effective in protecting against deep vein thrombosis (DVT). One group of patients will be given the medication, while the control group will be given a placebo. We not only have to measure whether the medication is more effective (are there fewer DVTs in the group given the medication?) but also the costs and (if one wants to make a comparison with the cost-effectiveness of interventions in other disease areas) the QALYs in both groups. Therefore, within the context of the clinical study we also collect economic and quality of life data. This is sometimes referred to as a 'piggy-back' study. However, this approach runs up against a number of problems (see Baker et al. and Mauskopf et al.[33][34]):

- **Protocol-induced costs**: it is typical of a clinical study that a protocol is imposed on the participating doctors or care providers to determine how the patient must be treated, how often they have to see the patient, what examinations have to be carried out, and at which frequency, which investigations should not be carried out, and so on. If the medical consumption patterns (and hence the costs) are to be measured within the context of this protocol, one is actually measuring what one imposed oneself in the protocol!

- **Protocol-induced findings**: even worse, because certain examinations are imposed, there will be findings which would not occur in reality outside the context of the study. In the case of prevention of DVT, the clinical study may oblige the participating doctors to carry out a venography for every patient because this is the most objective way of examining whether there is a DVT. However, in the real world of daily practice, venography is not carried out for everyone and DVTs are sometimes missed (for instance when they are not symptomatic). The study in which the venography is carried out will therefore lead to findings which will in turn result in medical actions (resulting both in health effects and costs) which would not occur in reality. It is then said that the study has a poor 'external validity'.

- **Exclusion of patients**: in clinical studies exclusion criteria are always used to ensure that the population being studied is sufficiently uniform and that there are no disruptive factors. For exam-

---

[33] Baker A et al. Considerations in measuring resource use in clinical trials. Drug information Journal 1995, Vol 29: 1421-1428.
[34] Mauskopf J et al. A strategy for collecting pharmacoeconomic data during phase II/III clinical trials. PharmacoEconomics 1996, 9(3): 264-277.

ple, patients with too much co-morbidity and patients with cognitive problems will typically be excluded. Again, this results in a distorted picture when average medical consumption and costs are based solely on the remaining patients.

- **The alternative treatment**: in clinical studies the control group is often given a placebo. After all, the aim is to find out whether the active product (in our example: heparins) actually has an effect in addition to the placebo. However, in the real situation the alternative in this example of prevention of DVT post discharge is not a placebo, but 'doing nothing' (or applying stockings). In other situations, the alternative is, for instance, the drug most used currently, or the current medical approach to a patient, consisting of a mix of therapies. Again this leads to problems if one wishes to determine the real medical consumption and costs in the context of a prospective clinical trial where the comparator is a placebo.

- **Terminating the study**: when a patient reaches an endpoint in a study (e.g., a complication) the study is usually terminated for that patient. In our example, most protocols for clinical studies will state that a patient in whom a DVT has been found will not usually have to continue participating in this study. In this way we miss the crucial information on how this DVT was treated and what medical consumption arises from this.

- **Time horizon**: even if all the patients are successfully kept in the study with clear instructions in the protocol in this respect, the question is still how long the study should last. In our example of preventing DVT, in order to draw some clinical conclusions a number of weeks are probably enough: after three weeks of the medication it will be possible to determine whether there is a difference in the rate of DVTs in the two groups. But what about the economic consequences? After all, it is possible that patients with a DVT have a greater chance of later developing a recurrent DVT. Perhaps they also have a chance of developing the so-called post-thrombotic syndrome (also called the post-phlebitic syndrome). Should these patients therefore be followed up over a period of years to find this out and should one measure the consequences with regard to medical consumption and costs for such a long time period? Obviously this is not feasible because it would not only be very expensive to do but would also take years before it would be possible to draw a conclusion with regard to cost and effectiveness.

The above problems help explain why health economic evaluations which are based on clinical studies are not very common. However, in situations where it has been possible to mimic the real world as closely as possible, this sort of study is feasible.

In carrying out such studies, the following recommendations will help:

1. Endeavour to keep to as 'thin' a protocol as possible: impose as few consultations, interventions and examinations as possible in the study. After all, the intention is to imitate reality. For example, if a patient with depression is usually seen after two weeks and then after eight weeks, there is no point in organising a weekly visit in the context of the study.

2. Integrate the questions on the economic data (medical consumption) in the forms for data collection (the CRF or Case Report Form). There is no point in dealing with all these questions in a separate questionnaire. It is better to not only collect the clinical information when the patient is seen in the context of the study, but also to find out at the same time what medical consumption there has been since the last visit.

3. Only collect information on medical consumption which is related to the disease and its treatment. For example, a study on the treatment of patients with a coronary condition using antihypertensive drugs should only collect data related to the treatment (drugs, consultations, hospitalisation, medicines, etc.) of that condition and the possible side effects of the drugs. This maxim may seem obvious in principle, but in practice it is not always that simple.

4. Make every attempt to continue monitoring the medical consumption of the 'drop-outs', for example by contacting these patients subsequently and asking them to send the relevant information in a prepaid envelope.

It should be noted that no matter how well this sort of prospective study is designed and how closely it imitates reality, both the patient and the provider are still influenced by the mere fact that they are consciously participating in a study. Because of this consciousness, both the behaviour of the patient and that of the care provider will be different from their behaviour outside the context of the study. This is known as the Hawthorne effect. The interested reader is referred to Mangione-Smith et al.[35]

3.1.2 Retrospective health economic evaluations

Are there more possibilities in a retrospective health economic evaluation? In this sort of evaluation one looks back and studies the clinical and economic consequences of patients who once started treatment 'A' and others who once started treatment 'B'. For example, A could be usual care for chronic lower back pain with a combination of medication and physiotherapy, while B involves an intensive rehabilitation programme. There is certainly no Hawthorne effect here because the treatments did not take place in the context of a study. It is only at a later date that the decision is made to observe what happened. Furthermore there are no protocol-induced costs or findings (see previous section). In addition, it is possible to study a population of patients who are given the treatment in the real situation and where the alternative treatment does not contain a placebo.

But there are four important disadvantages of this method:

1. The treatment allocation did not take place in a randomised way. This means that there is a large chance that the patients who received treatment A have characteristics that are different from those who received treatment B. Perhaps the expectations with regard to B were high and it was particularly the seriously ill patients who were given this treatment. Or possibly the family situation of those who were given treatment B was different from those who received A. This problem is known as confounding, more specifically *selection bias*. [36] The result of selection bias is that when there is a difference in the effects and costs between A and B, one does not know whether this difference is due to the difference in treatment itself or to the difference in the characteristics between the patients who received A and those who received B. There are statistical methods to correct the results for the differ-

---

[35] Mangione-Smith R, Elliott MN, McDonald L, McGlynn EA. An observational study of antibiotic prescribing behavior and the Hawthorne effect. Health Serv Res. 2002 Dec;37(6):1603-23.

[36] Motheral B, Brooks J, Clark MA, Crown WH, Davey P, Hutchins D, Martin BC, Stang P. A checklist for retrospective database studies—report of the ISPOR Task Force on Retrospective Databases. Value Health. 2003 Mar-Apr;6(2):90-7.

ences in characteristics, but this is only possible for the known differences - some are likely to be unknown.

2. The data are incomplete: they are based entirely on data from the medical files or insurance claims of the patients concerned. These files may be incomplete and/or contain incorrect information, so that the results of the evaluation will not provide a correct reflection of reality.

3. The timeframe: this sort of retrospective health economic evaluation can be carried out only when a treatment has been 'on the market' for quite a while. After all, it is only then that it is possible to look back at patients who once started the treatment. In other words, this method cannot be applied for new technologies or treatments.

4. Finally, the retrospective technique does not make it possible to measure quality of life because it is obviously not customary to measure this in reality – in contrast with a clinical study – for example, on the basis of an EQ-5D.

Therefore we can conclude that neither the prospective nor the retrospective methods are ideal methods to serve as the basis for health economic evaluations. They can of course be applied, but then one has to account for the abovementioned disadvantages.

3.2 The decision model: general calculation principles

The decision model has a major role in the world of health economic evaluations. And the concept is quite simple as well. The decision maker has to make a decision whether treatment A or treatment B is preferable for a particular patient type on the basis of our two dimensions: costs and health effects. Figure 11 shows a simple example in which only the costs are examined. This is not really a complete health economic evaluation (for which it is necessary to examine both dimensions), but I want to start with this simple example.

The example concerns the treatment of patients with chronic lower back pain. For the sake of simplicity, the costs of treatments A and B are shown at the top of the figure as €1,000 and €2,000 respectively and the cost in case of treatment failure is shown as €10,000 (which may be explained by the fact that the patient needs to be hospitalized and/or has to undergo surgery). In reality the health economist has to measure and calculate these values. For the cost of a medicine this is usually the cost per day (taking into account the dose per day, the cost of a pack and the number of doses per pack) multiplied by the number of days of treatment. For the cost of the failure of the therapy, various sources can be used (see below).

In this example, the purchase cost of treatment B is twice as high as that of treatment A. But extra information is given in the figure as well: with B there is a chance of failure of only 10%, while this is 30% for A. These figures (the chance of success and the chance of failure) are usually taken from the literature or from a clinical trial report. So, in the case of treatment A, there is a 30% chance of this large cost of €10,000, while in the case of therapy B the chance is only 10%. We can now calculate the *expected* cost of A and B. This is done on the basis of the *weighted average*: every scenario is assigned a weight depending on how often it can occur.

For A the weighted average is 0.7 x €1,000 + 0.3 x (€1,000+€10,000) = €700 + €3,300 = **€4,000**.

For B this is 0.9 x €2,000 + 0.1 x (€2,000 + €10,000) = €1,800 + €1,200 = **€3,000**.

Figure 11: Example of a decision tree with a calculation of the expected costs

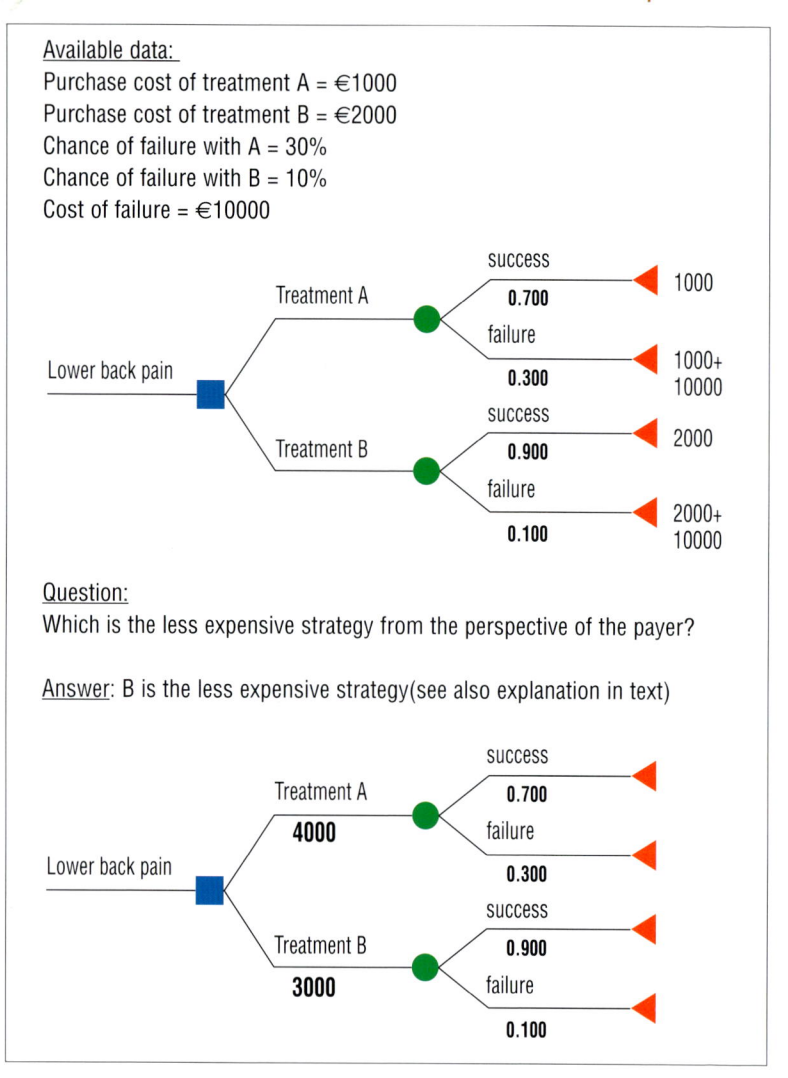

Available data:
Purchase cost of treatment A = €1000
Purchase cost of treatment B = €2000
Chance of failure with A = 30%
Chance of failure with B = 10%
Cost of failure = €10000

```
                                    success
                    Treatment A      0.700      → 1000
Lower back pain  ──┤              ──┤
                                    failure    → 1000+
                                    0.300        10000

                                    success
                    Treatment B      0.900      → 2000
                   ──┤              ──┤
                                    failure    → 2000+
                                    0.100        10000
```

Question:
Which is the less expensive strategy from the perspective of the payer?

Answer: B is the less expensive strategy (see also explanation in text)

```
                    Treatment A      success
                       4000          0.700
                   ──┤              ──┤
Lower back pain                       failure
                                      0.300

                    Treatment B      success
                       3000          0.900
                   ──┤              ──┤
                                      failure
                                      0.100
```

Despite the larger purchase cost, B is a less expensive choice overall in this example. Therefore a policy maker/payer will normally opt for B.

For the reader who needs to learn more about the concept of a weighted average, the box text below contains further details.

> ### Weighted average: workings in detail:
>
> Consider the example of treatment A. The chance of success is 0.7 (7 chances out of 10) and the chance of failure is 0.3 (3 chances out of 10). In the case of success, the total cost is €1,000 (only the cost of treatment); in the case of failure, the total cost is €11,000 (€1,000 for the treatment and €10,000 for the failure).
>
> If 10 patients are treated with A, the expectation is that 7 will have a successful treatment while the treatment will fail for 3 patients.
>
> The cost of these 10 patients together is €40,000:
>
> | | |
> |---|---|
> | Patient 1 (success) | €1,000 |
> | Patient 2 (success) | €1,000 |
> | Patient 3 (success) | €1,000 |
> | Patient 4 (success) | €1,000 |
> | Patient 5 (success) | €1,000 |
> | Patient 6 (success) | €1,000 |
> | Patient 7 (success) | €1,000 |
> | Patient 8 (failure) | €11,000 |
> | Patient 9 (failure) | €11,000 |
> | Patient 10 (failure) | €11,000 |
> | TOTAL | €40,000 |
>
> The average cost per patient is therefore €40,000/10 = €4,000.

Figure 12 shows a second example, looking this time not only at costs but also at effects. This example concerns the prevention of a heart attack (myocardial infarction; MI) in patients with a high risk of coronary heart disease (CHD). The chance of an MI (e.g. over a period of 10 years) is 30% if no preventive action is taken. With prevention, the chance drops to 20%. The cost of an MI is €10,000. The number of expected QALYs in the case of an MI is only 6, while this number is 10 without MI.

Figure 12: Example of a decision tree with calculation of expected costs and effects.

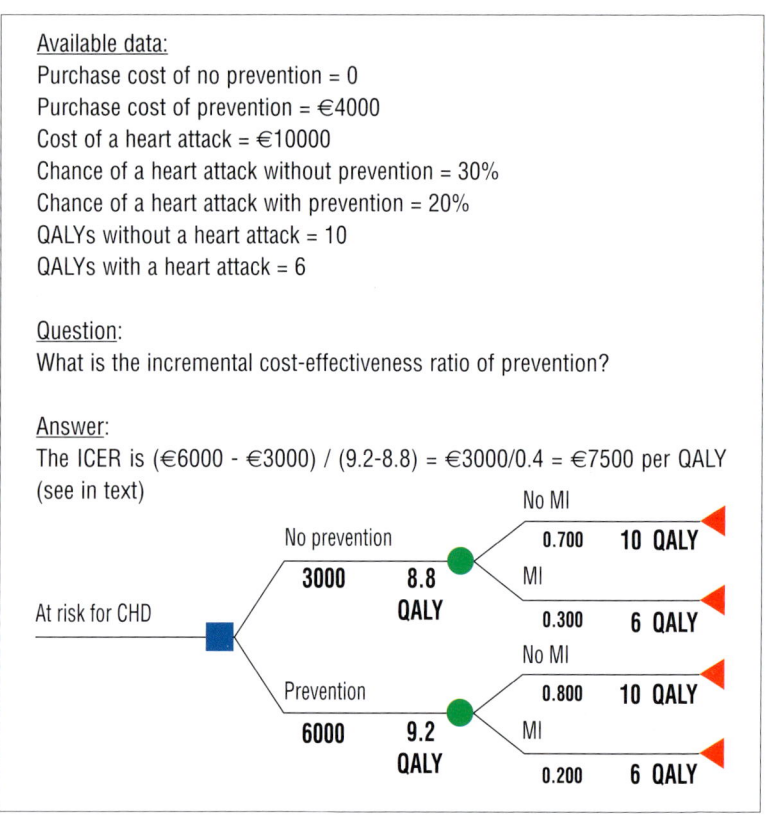

Available data:
Purchase cost of no prevention = 0
Purchase cost of prevention = €4000
Cost of a heart attack = €10000
Chance of a heart attack without prevention = 30%
Chance of a heart attack with prevention = 20%
QALYs without a heart attack = 10
QALYs with a heart attack = 6

Question:
What is the incremental cost-effectiveness ratio of prevention?

Answer:
The ICER is (€6000 - €3000) / (9.2-8.8) = €3000/0.4 = €7500 per QALY (see in text)

```
                    No prevention             No MI
                                              0.700    10 QALY
                       3000      8.8
                                 QALY         MI
At risk for CHD                               0.300    6 QALY
                                              No MI
                    Prevention                0.800    10 QALY
                       6000      9.2
                                 QALY         MI
                                              0.200    6 QALY
```

CHD = coronary heart disease

The expected (weighted average) cost is now:

0.7 x 0 + 0.3 x €10,000 = **€3,000** without prevention, and
0.8 x €4,000 + 0.2 x €14,000 = €3,200 + €2,800 = **€6,000** with prevention.

Thus prevention is a more expensive strategy than no prevention. In fact, this is often the case. On closer inspection it is not illogical. After all, the absolute difference between the chance of a heart attack is only 0.1 (or 10%). In other words, if the prevention is used for 10 people this will only make a difference for one of them: without prevention 3 would have a heart attack, and with prevention only 2. We must carry out prevention for 10 people in order to help just one of

them. This figure is known as the _Number Needed to Treat_
Note that in the first example, Figure 11, the absolute risk
(ARR) was 20% (from 30% with treatment A to 10% with treatment B). Hence, the NNT was 5 (it needs 10 patients to be treated in order to avoid 2 failures → 5 to avoid 1 failure). Technically, the NNT = 1/ARR. In the example of Figure 11: 1/20% = 1/0.2 = 5.

However, there is also our second dimension and our goal of health care (and prevention): to achieve health gains.
Without prevention, the expected health effect in Figure 12 is 0.7 x 10 + 0.3 x 6 = **8.8 QALYs**.
With prevention this is 0.8 x 10 + 0.2 x 6 = **9.2 QALYs**. Thus, we gain 0.4 QALYs!
The ICER is then the ratio of the net cost of prevention to the net gain in health:

ICER = (€6,000-€3,000) / (9.2 – 8.8) = €3,000 / 0.4 = **€7,500/QALY**.
In other words: we spend €3,000 to gain 0.4 QALYs. This amounts to €750 to gain 0.1 QALY and so €7,500 to gain 1 QALY. In the ICER, the denominator is always equal to 1 QALY so that different investments in health care can, in principle, be compared.

In this case we can conclude that prevention may not actually save costs, but that it is cost-effective if we accept that the threshold of willingness to pay for a QALY fluctuates at around €30,000 per QALY (see Chapter 2, section 2.5).

Note that the cost to prevent one MI can also be calculated, namely €3,000/0.1 = €30,000 per avoided MI. As explained above, decision makers who are interested in reducing the number of MIs in a country or region and in how to best spend the money to achieve that goal may be more interested in the cost per prevented MI rather than in the cost per QALY.

In the next and last example, we look at the same type of patient, but this time we assume that the risk of MI is only 12% without prevention and that this risk can be reduced by prevention to 8%. The absolute gain is therefore 4%. The NNT = 1/0.04 = 25.
Figure 13 shows this example. The cost of a heart attack is still €10,000 and the number of expected QALYs in the case of a heart attack is 6, while it is 10 without a heart attack. The expected cost is now:

0.88 x 0 + 0.12 x €10,000 = **€1,200** without prevention, and
0.92 x €4,000 + 0.08 x €14,000 = €3,680 + €1,120 = **€4,800** with prevention.
Therefore prevention is once again a more expensive strategy than no prevention: the net cost amounts to €4,800 minus €1,200 = €3,600.

However, we again gain QALYs. Without prevention the expected gain is 0.88 x 10 + 0.12 x 6 = **9.52 QALYs**. With prevention, this is 0.92 x 10 + 0.08 x 6 = **9.68 QALYs**, a difference of 0.16 with no prevention.

The ICER is €3,600 / (9.68 – 9.52) = €3,600 / 0.16 = **€22,500/QALY**. If the threshold of willingness to pay for a QALY fluctuates around €30,000, the result of this decision tree is still under the threshold, but it comes close to it: therefore, it cannot really be called *very* cost-effective, but it cannot be considered as too expensive either. The policy makers will now have to decide whether they want to pay for this prevention and their decision will depend on several factors other than this ICER. I return to this in the last chapter.

A final note on the NNT: a better (lower) NNT is generally, but not necessarily associated with a better ICER. If the treatment is very expensive, and the avoided failure is very cheap and does not have a strong impact on a patient's quality of life, the ICER may still be very high (= bad).

Figure 13: Example of a decision tree with calculation of expected costs and effects (2).

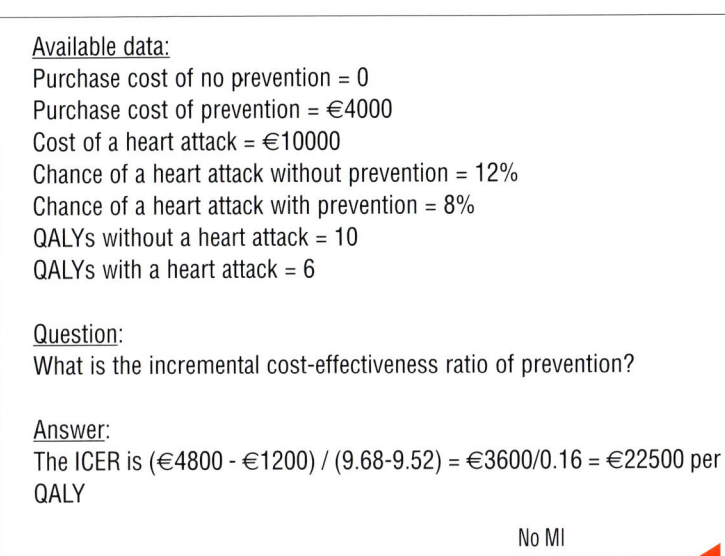

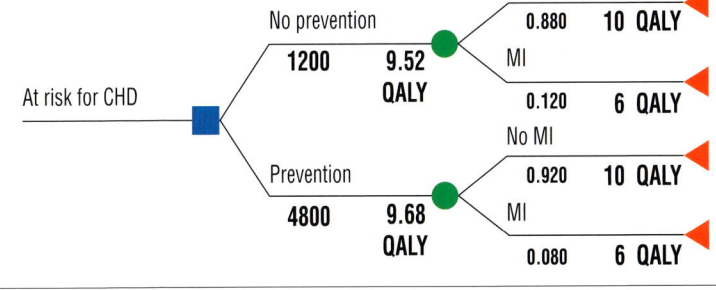

Available data:
Purchase cost of no prevention = 0
Purchase cost of prevention = €4000
Cost of a heart attack = €10000
Chance of a heart attack without prevention = 12%
Chance of a heart attack with prevention = 8%
QALYs without a heart attack = 10
QALYs with a heart attack = 6

Question:
What is the incremental cost-effectiveness ratio of prevention?

Answer:
The ICER is (€4800 - €1200) / (9.68-9.52) = €3600/0.16 = €22500 per QALY

```
                                          No MI
                    No prevention          0.880    10 QALY
                    1200      9.52
                              QALY        MI
At risk for CHD                            0.120     6 QALY
                                          No MI
                    Prevention             0.920    10 QALY
                    4800      9.68
                              QALY        MI
                                           0.080     6 QALY
```

CHD = coronary heart disease

3.3 A real example: the prevention of deep vein thrombosis (DVT)

3.3.1 Introduction

In reality the decision trees which are used for health economic evaluations are obviously more complex than the decision trees in the previous section. In order to reveal what really happens in this sort of evaluation, we will examine here an example (inspired by a study by Haentjens et al. [37]) on the cost-effectiveness of prolonged prophylaxis (after being discharged from hospital) with low molecular weight heparins (LMWH) after a total hip or knee replacement.

The question is whether this prolonged prophylaxis is cost-effective. This question is relevant because after being discharged from hospital there is still a significant risk of DVT. This risk (symptomatic and asymptomatic together) is about 35%. It should be noted that for the sake of simplicity, no distinction is made here between proximal and distal DVT. It should also be noted that obviously not all DVTs are symptomatic. (On average only 25% of DVTs are symptomatic and thus identified.)

3.3.2 The DVT decision tree

The question can be answered with the use of a decision tree. Figure 14 illustrates this tree. It should be noted that we start with the distinction DVT/no DVT. In reality, the treating physician does not know who has a DVT. However, on the basis of published studies or clinical study reports, the designers (as well as the readers) of the model know what percentage of patients will have a DVT - in our example this is 35% - and also what percentage of the patients with a DVT are symptomatic - in our example, 25%. This 25% is a conditional probability: *if* there is a DVT, the chance that this is symptomatic is equal to 25%. Overall, the chance of a symptomatic DVT is equal to 25% of 35%, i.e. 0.25 x 0.35 =0.0875 (8.75%).

---

[37] Haentjens P, De Groote K, Annemans L. Prolonged enoxaparin therapy to prevent venous thromboembolism after primary hip or knee replacement. A cost-utility analysis. Arch Orthop Trauma Surg. 2004 Oct;124(8):507-17.

In the case of a symptomatic DVT, an echography will be carried out. If this is positive, treatment will be started. Despite the treatment there is still a chance, admittedly a very small one, of a pulmonary embolism (PE) which may be fatal. We assume that if the echography is negative, a venography will be carried out. We also assume that the venography will give the correct result in 100% of cases and will therefore lead to the treatment of the DVT (after all, we are still in the part of the decision tree where there is a DVT). Whether the treatment is successful or not, the patient eventually has the chance of a recurrent DVT as well as a PTS (post-thrombotic syndrome).

If the DVT is not symptomatic or is not identified, there will obviously also be a chance of a PE which may be fatal. And once again, there is a chance of a recurrent DVT and of a PTS, although it is typical of asymptomatic DVTs that these chances are now smaller.

In the case that there is no DVT, nothing further happens (in reality, this is more complex, because in the absence of a DVT, there may be 'DVT-like' symptoms). In total 22 scenarios can arise, as indicated in the figure. The figure only shows the branch for the strategy 'no prophylaxis'. The strategy 'prolonged prophylaxis' has the same structure.

Figure 14: Decision tree for the analysis of the cost-effectiveness of prolonged prophylaxis against deep vein thrombosis (DVT)

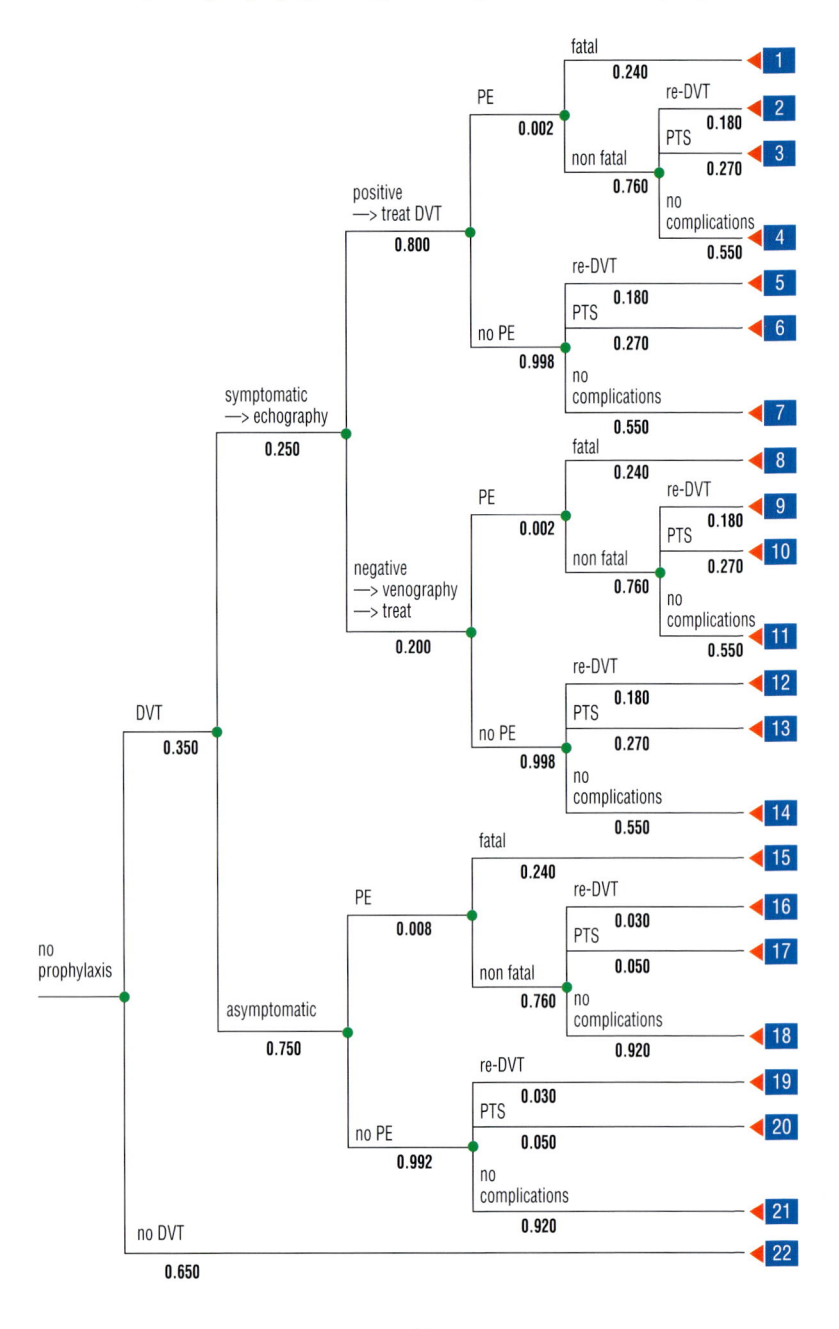

3.3.3 Probabilities

The previous section has already indicated some probabilities applicable to this tree, which are also shown in the above figure. Table 2 provides a summary of the different probabilities in which only the probability of a DVT is determined by the strategy that is chosen (see first 2 rows of the table), and the other probabilities are the same for both branches of the tree. Hence, only the probability of a DVT is influenced by the better strategy. But once the patient has a DVT, the remainder of the process is no longer determined by the original preventive strategy.

Table 2: Probabilities in the decision tree related to prophylaxis of DVT.

Event	Probability
DVT without further prophylaxis	*0.35*
DVT with prolonged prophylaxis	*0.20*
Clinical symptoms in case of DVT	0.25
Sensitivity of echography*	0.80
Sensitivity of venography*	1.00
Recurrent DVT within a year if the original DVT was symptomatic	0.18
Recurrent of DVT within a year if the original DVT was asymptomatic	0.03
Post-thrombotic syndrome (PTS)	
After symptomatic DVT	0.27
After asymptomatic DVT	0.05
PE after DVT if the DVT was not treated	0.008
PE after DVT if the DVT was treated	0.002
Mortality as a result of PE	0.24

* The sensitivity of a test indicates the probability that if the patient has the disease, the test will be positive. For instance, a sensitivity of 0.8 means that 80% of all DVTs will be identified by the test.

3.3.4 Costs and QALYs

When the structure of the tree has been determined and data on the probabilities have been collected, measurements and calculations are made of the costs and health effects for each scenario. In the study which inspired this example (Haentjens et al.), these data were collected on the basis of three types of sources:

- Already existing publications
- Analysis of patient files
- Interviews with doctors

For example, if the cost of a PTS has been very recently published, the effort of calculating that cost obviously does not have to be made again. However, if no such publication exists, an analysis can be carried out of medical files of patients or insurance claims (if they contain the information) and the average cost can be determined on this basis. If neither the time nor the budget are available for this, or the data are lacking, then (as a kind of 'last resort') an interview with care providers can be conducted to ascertain how this type of patient is being treated. The most commonly used method for this last procedure is known as the Delphi technique. [38]

A summary of the costs in the model is shown in Table 3. The expected health, expressed here in QALYs, is also measured and established for each scenario. These QALY weights are also shown in Table 3. The box text below explains the Delphi technique in more detail.

Table 3: Costs and QALYs for every scenario of the model

Scenario or event	Cost (€)	Effect on the QALY weight
Prophylaxis for 3 weeks after discharge	€130	-
Venography	€60	
Symptomatic DVT (including echography)	€1500	-0.16 for 3 months
Re-DVT	€1500	-0.16 for 3 months
PE	€4000	-0.24 for 6 months
PTS	€200	-0.07 for 9 months

---

[38] Evans C, Crawford B. Expert judgement in pharmacoeconomic studies. Guidance and future use. Pharmacoeconomics. 2000 Jun;17(6):545-53.

The Delphi technique

Suppose that the Delphi technique is to be used to determine the cost of a DVT. A number of physicians or care providers are selected (usually about 10-12 suffices) and they are asked questions about medical consumption related to the diagnosis (which tests are conducted and how many) and the treatment (what medication, how much and how long) for this problem in well defined patients and in well defined conditions. The care providers are usually surveyed in writing, in a number of rounds. After the first round of questions the results are summarised (e.g. on the basis of the average of the various respondents and the minimum and maximum figures). These results of the first round are then presented again to all the participants and they are asked to reconsider their original responses. Experience shows that after the second round, results are closer together and usually also closer to reality.[38] Note that the Delphi technique only aims at collecting data on medical resource use. Afterwards, once the medical consumption is known, every element of it is multiplied by its unit cost. For example, it may be found that for 50% of the patients, an X-ray of the thorax is taken, and it is known that this sort of test costs €25, so that the expected cost of this element = 0.5 x €25 = €12.5.

The Delphi technique is much less reliable than an analysis based on individual patient data because it is obviously dependent on the *estimates* of the care provider concerned with regard to *average* medical consumption.

Finally, an important note related to the calculation of QALYs in the tree. We have seen before that the weight of a health condition (the utility) that is used to calculate the number of QALYs is expressed as a value between 0 and 1. For a 'bad' event (a complication or side effect) a 'QALY penalty' is often assigned, i.e. a loss of QALY.[39] This works as follows. If the patient is in a scenario without complications, he/she will receive a basic QALY weight corresponding to the average age of the patient concerned. This basic figure is not equal to 1, but lower. In our example we assume that this basic figure is 0.85. This means that the average patient with a total hip replacement and without complications has a quality weight ('utility level') of 0.85. However, as soon as there are complications, the patient temporarily loses a certain amount of quality of life. For example, Table 3 indi-

---

[39] see for instance Wirt DP, et al. Cost-Effectiveness of interferon alfa-2b added to chemotherapy for high-tumor-burden follicular non-Hodgkin's lymphoma. Leuk Lymphoma. 2001 Feb;40(5-6):565-79

cates that a DVT leads to a loss of 0.16 (on the scale between 0 and 1) for 3 months. Now, since 3 months = 0.25 years this means a loss of 0.16 x 0.25 = 0.04 QALYs.

Publications can serve as a source here, but a separate study can also be carried out in order to measure the utility level of the different conditions, for instance on the basis of an EQ-5D (see section 2.4.3.).

3.3.5 Calculating the decision tree

We now have all the information available to calculate the tree. The final result will show a weighted average cost and a weighted average health effect for both strategies, prolonged prophylaxis compared with no further prophylaxis post discharge. This result is shown in Figures 15A and B (no further medication) and 16 A and B (further medication after discharge).

The concept is the same again: every scenario has a final probability, a final cost and a final number of QALYs. The result of a particular strategy is equal to the weighted average of the different scenarios:

> *Weighted cost = cost of scenario 1 x probability of scenario 1 + cost of scenario 2 x probability of scenario 2 + …cost of scenario 22 x probability of scenario 22.*

> *Weighted QALYs = QALY of scenario 1 x probability of scenario 1 + QALY of scenario 2 x probability of scenario 2 + … QALY of scenario 22 x probability of scenario 22.*

Part A of each figure shows the probabilities of all the scenarios (see the P figures on the right of the figure); part B shows the costs per scenario and the weighted average cost, as well as the QALYs per scenario and the weighted average number of QALYs. Do not forget that time is taken into account for the calculation of the number of QALYs: e.g., the loss of QALYs as a result of the DVT is 0.16 x 3 months = 0.16 x 3/12 years = 0.04 QALY.

3 Methods for economic evaluations

Figure 15 A: Probability of every scenario for the strategy 'no prophylaxis'

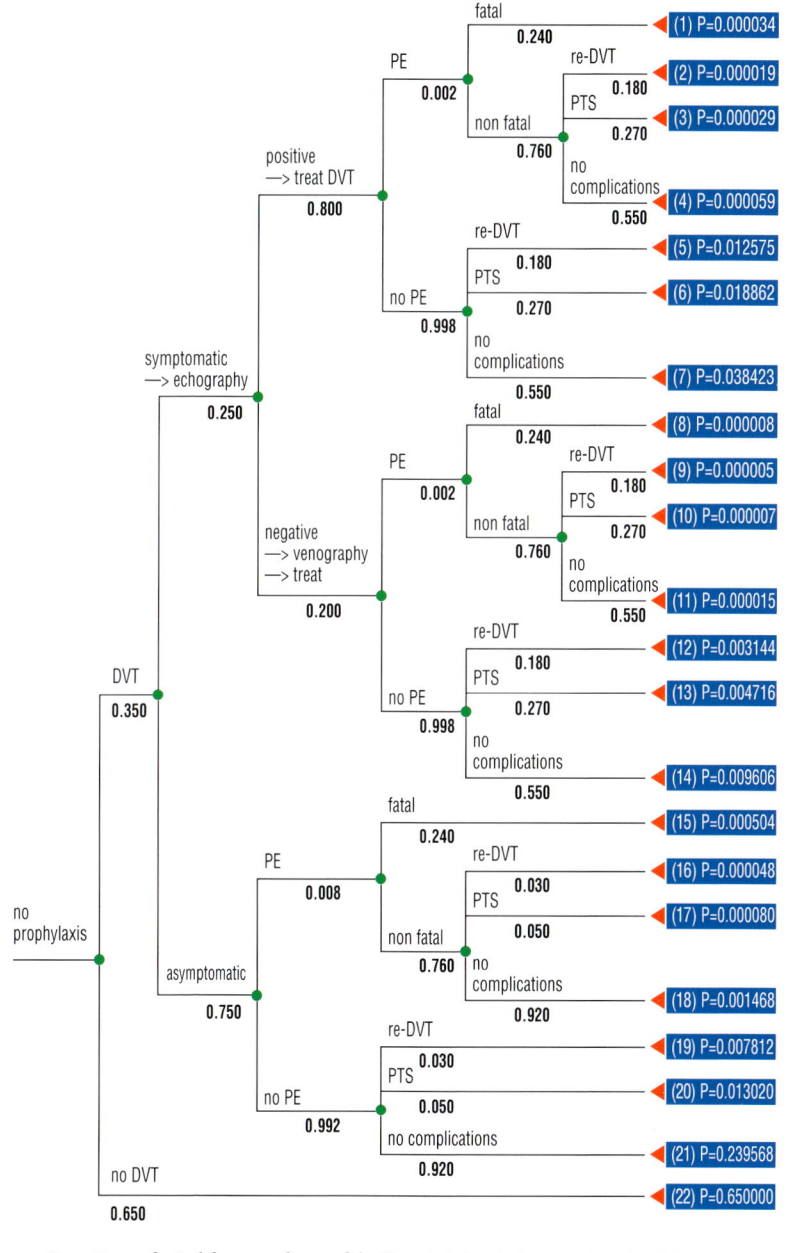

```
no prophylaxis
├── DVT (0.350)
│   ├── symptomatic → echography (0.250)
│   │   ├── positive → treat DVT (0.800)
│   │   │   ├── PE (0.002)
│   │   │   │   ├── fatal (0.240) ──────────────────────── (1) P=0.000034
│   │   │   │   └── non fatal (0.760)
│   │   │   │       ├── re-DVT (0.180) ─────────────────── (2) P=0.000019
│   │   │   │       ├── PTS (0.270) ─────────────────────── (3) P=0.000029
│   │   │   │       └── no complications (0.550) ────────── (4) P=0.000059
│   │   │   └── no PE (0.998)
│   │   │       ├── re-DVT (0.180) ─────────────────────── (5) P=0.012575
│   │   │       ├── PTS (0.270) ─────────────────────────── (6) P=0.018862
│   │   │       └── no complications (0.550) ────────────── (7) P=0.038423
│   │   └── negative → venography → treat (0.200)
│   │       ├── PE (0.002)
│   │       │   ├── fatal (0.240) ──────────────────────── (8) P=0.000008
│   │       │   └── non fatal (0.760)
│   │       │       ├── re-DVT (0.180) ─────────────────── (9) P=0.000005
│   │       │       ├── PTS (0.270) ────────────────────── (10) P=0.000007
│   │       │       └── no complications (0.550) ───────── (11) P=0.000015
│   │       └── no PE (0.998)
│   │           ├── re-DVT (0.180) ─────────────────────── (12) P=0.003144
│   │           ├── PTS (0.270) ────────────────────────── (13) P=0.004716
│   │           └── no complications (0.550) ───────────── (14) P=0.009606
│   └── asymptomatic (0.750)
│       ├── PE (0.008)
│       │   ├── fatal (0.240) ──────────────────────────── (15) P=0.000504
│       │   └── non fatal (0.760)
│       │       ├── re-DVT (0.030) ─────────────────────── (16) P=0.000048
│       │       ├── PTS (0.050) ────────────────────────── (17) P=0.000080
│       │       └── no complications (0.920) ───────────── (18) P=0.001468
│       └── no PE (0.992)
│           ├── re-DVT (0.030) ─────────────────────────── (19) P=0.007812
│           ├── PTS (0.050) ────────────────────────────── (20) P=0.013020
│           └── no complications (0.920) ───────────────── (21) P=0.239568
└── no DVT (0.650) ───────────────────────────────────── (22) P=0.650000
```

E.g. Branch 1 (the top branch): P = 0.35 x 0.25 x 0.8 x 0.002 x 0.24 = 0.000034

Figure 15 B: Costs and QALYs for every scenario and weighted average cost and QALYs for the strategy 'no prophylaxis'

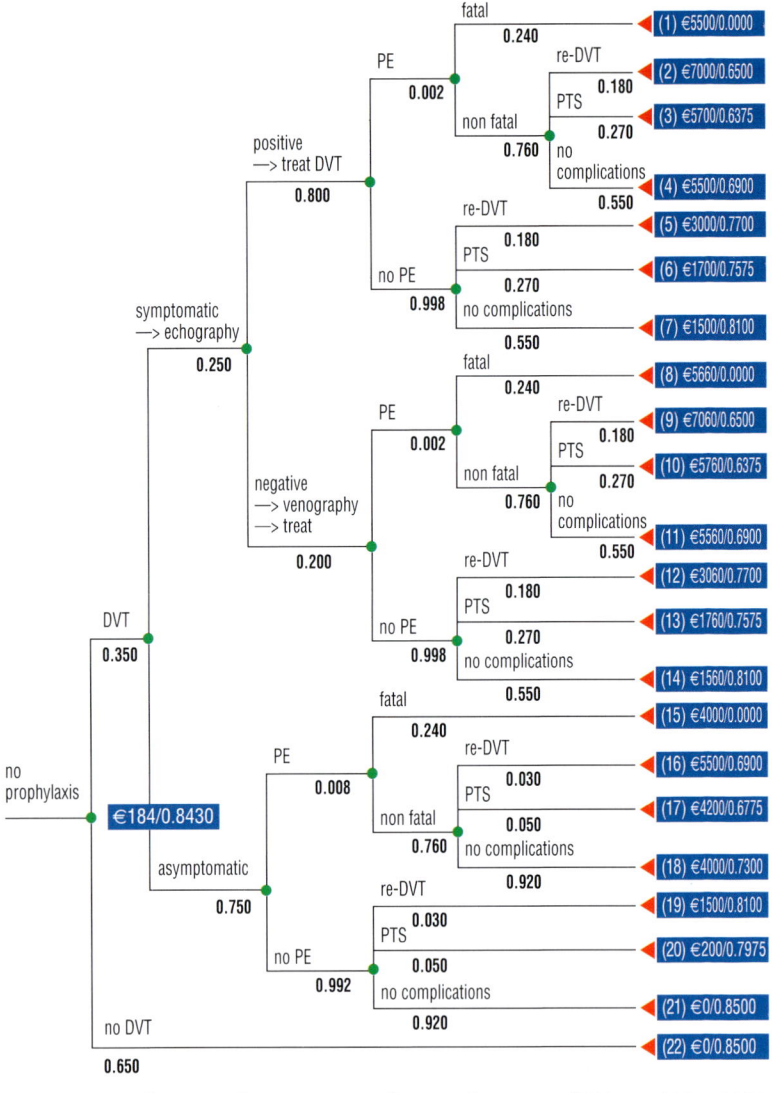

E.g. Branch 1: total cost = cost of DVT plus cost of PE = 1500 + 4000 = 5500

E.g. Branch 2: total cost = cost of DVT plus cost of PE plus cost of re-DVT = 1500 + 4000 + 1500 = 7000

E.g. Branch 2: QALYs = 0.85 − 3/12 x 0.16 − 6/12 x 0.24 − 3/12 x 0.16 = 0.85 − 0.04 − 0.12 − 0.04 = 0.65

3 Methods for economic evaluations

Figure 16 A: Probablity of every scenario for the strategy 'prolonged prophylaxis'

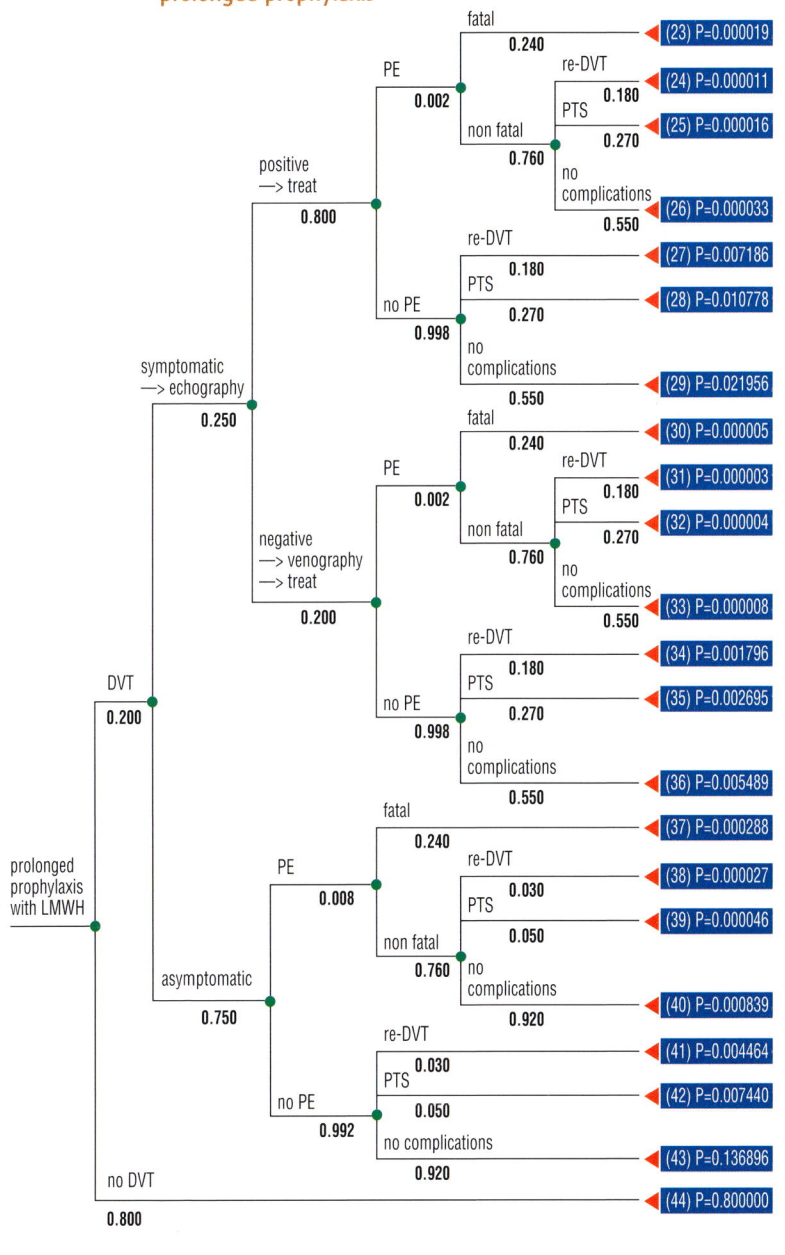

```
prolonged prophylaxis with LMWH
├── DVT (0.200)
│   ├── symptomatic → echography (0.250)
│   │   ├── positive → treat (0.800)
│   │   │   ├── PE (0.002)
│   │   │   │   ├── fatal (0.240) ──────────────── (23) P=0.000019
│   │   │   │   └── non fatal (0.760)
│   │   │   │       ├── re-DVT (0.180) ─────────── (24) P=0.000011
│   │   │   │       ├── PTS (0.270) ────────────── (25) P=0.000016
│   │   │   │       └── no complications (0.550) ─ (26) P=0.000033
│   │   │   └── no PE (0.998)
│   │   │       ├── re-DVT (0.180) ─────────────── (27) P=0.007186
│   │   │       ├── PTS (0.270) ────────────────── (28) P=0.010778
│   │   │       └── no complications (0.550) ───── (29) P=0.021956
│   │   └── negative → venography → treat (0.200)
│   │       ├── PE (0.002)
│   │       │   ├── fatal (0.240) ──────────────── (30) P=0.000005
│   │       │   └── non fatal (0.760)
│   │       │       ├── re-DVT (0.180) ─────────── (31) P=0.000003
│   │       │       ├── PTS (0.270) ────────────── (32) P=0.000004
│   │       │       └── no complications (0.550) ─ (33) P=0.000008
│   │       └── no PE (0.998)
│   │           ├── re-DVT (0.180) ─────────────── (34) P=0.001796
│   │           ├── PTS (0.270) ────────────────── (35) P=0.002695
│   │           └── no complications (0.550) ───── (36) P=0.005489
│   └── asymptomatic (0.750)
│       ├── PE (0.008)
│       │   ├── fatal (0.240) ──────────────────── (37) P=0.000288
│       │   └── non fatal (0.760)
│       │       ├── re-DVT (0.030) ─────────────── (38) P=0.000027
│       │       ├── PTS (0.050) ────────────────── (39) P=0.000046
│       │       └── no complications (0.920) ───── (40) P=0.000839
│       └── no PE (0.992)
│           ├── re-DVT (0.030) ──────────────────── (41) P=0.004464
│           ├── PTS (0.050) ─────────────────────── (42) P=0.007440
│           └── no complications (0.920) ────────── (43) P=0.136896
└── no DVT (0.800) ─────────────────────────────── (44) P=0.800000
```

E.g. Branch 23: $P = 0.2 \times 0.25 \times 0.8 \times 0.002 \times 0.24 = 0.000019$

Figure 16 B: Costs and QALYs for every scenario and weighted average cost and QALYs for the strategy 'prolonged prophylaxis'

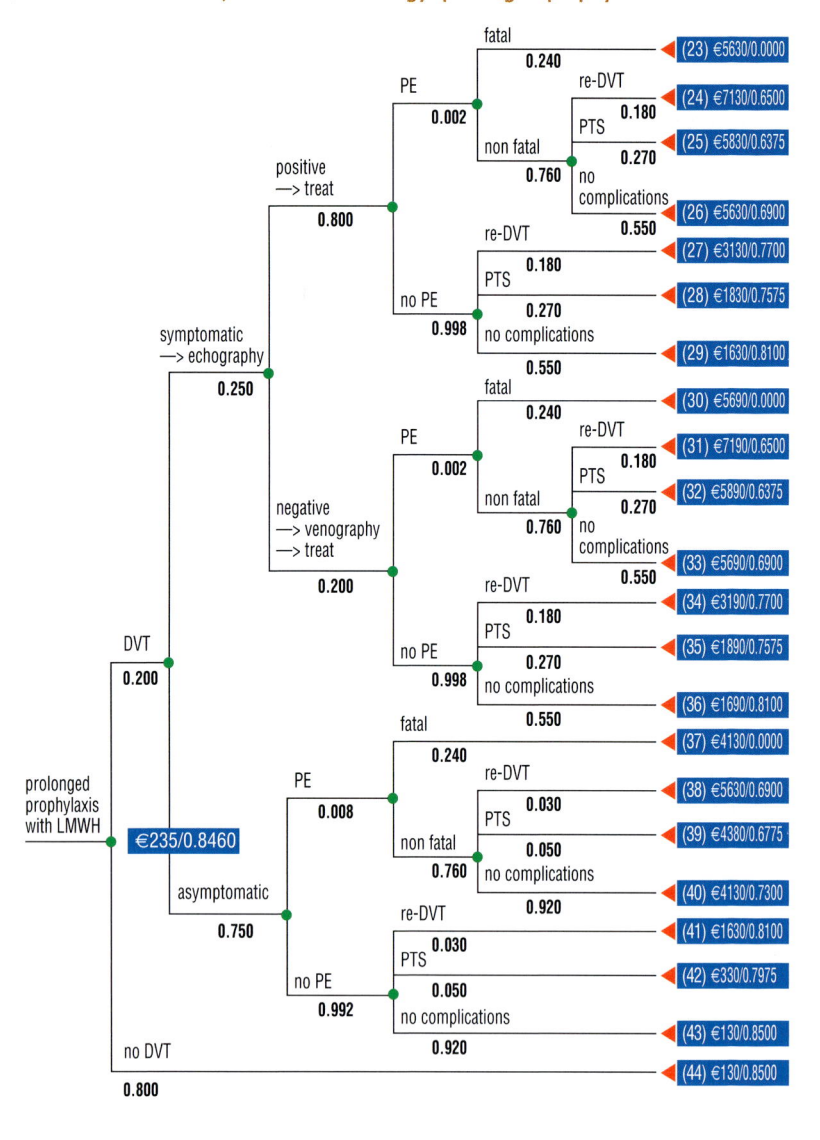

E.g. Branch 23: total cost = 130 +1500 + 4000 = 5630
E.g. Branch 24: total cost = 130 + 1500 + 4000 + 1500 = 7130
E.g. Branch 24: QALYs = 0.85 − 3/12 x 0.16 − 6/12 x 0.24 − 3/12 x 0.16 = 0.65

Table 4 contains a summary of the total costs and QALYs per strategy.
The expected cost without further prophylaxis = €184.1 (see rounded result at the root of the tree in Figure 15 B)
The expected cost with prolonged prophylaxis = €235.2 (see Figure 16B)
The expected number of QALYs without further prophylaxis is 0.84296 (Figure 15B)
The expected number of QALYs with prolonged prophylaxis is 0.84598 (Figure 16B)

→ The incremental cost-effectiveness ratio (ICER) amounts to: (€235.2 - €184.1) / (0.84598 - 0.84296) = €51.1 / 0.00302 = €16927 per QALY.

Assuming a threshold of €30,000 per QALY is used, this is a fairly acceptable result.

Table 4: Costs, QALYs and ICER of prolonged prophylaxis in comparison with no further prophylaxis

Strategy	Cost	Incremental Cost	Effect	Incremental Effect	ICER
No prophylaxis	€ 184.1		0.84296		
Prolonged prophylaxis	€ 235.2	€ 51.1	0.84598	0.00302	€ 16927

Further below we will look more closely at these results on the basis of a number of sensitivity analyses (see section 3.7). However, in the following section I first discuss the Markov model. This book does not deal with another – special – type of modelling, namely the Discrete Event Simulation type of modelling, in which every individual is considered separately and is characterised by features, risks and events during the course of the model (which follows a time clock). This form of modelling is not yet used very often, but could become more important in the future. The reader is referred to Caro (2005) for further details. [40]

---

[40] Caro JJ. Pharmacoeconomic analyses using discrete event simulation. Pharmacoeconomics. 2005;23(4):323-32.

3.4 The Markov model

The Markov model is a special form of decision model in which members of a population (which may be a population of patients, or a population of people for whom prevention is organised) are presumed to be at any point in time in one of several possible health or disease states. Over time, these people can evolve from one state to another. The evolution or transition from one state to another takes place with a particular probability (called the transition probability) and during fixed periods (called Markov cycles). The length of a cycle is determined in advance by the researcher.

A Markov model thus comprises 3 elements: [41]

- The possible states in which the patient can be
- The transition probabilities between the states
- The fixed period or cycle in which a transition probability applies. The total duration of a Markov model is the sum of the cycles.

More or less the simplest Markov model that can be imagined is one in which we consider 3 states: healthy, sick and dead. Everyone in the model starts in the 'healthy' state. Suppose that we start by looking at a cohort of 1,000 people. We define the fixed period (= cycle) as one year. We then decide (in this example) to look at three periods of one year. Thus, the total duration of the model is three years. Figure 17 shows the model with the transition probabilities per year. The probability per year that a healthy person will become sick is estimated to be 0.1. The annual probability of death for a healthy person is 0.01. A sick person has a probability of 0.2 of dying every year.

It is a requirement of a Markov model that only one transition per cycle is possible. It is not possible to fall sick and die in the same period. If this is possible in a real situation, the length of the period (cycle) has to be shortened so that this condition in the model of a maximum of one transition per period is maintained.

---

[41] Beck JR en Pauker SG. The Markov Process in Medical Prognosis. Med Decis Making, 1981, Vol 1 (4). See also the more recent Briggs A, Sculpher M. An introduction to Markov modelling for economic evaluation. Pharmacoeconomics 1998; 13(4): 397-409.

Figure 17: Simple Markov model with 3 health states

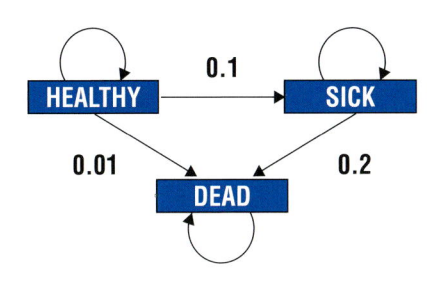

```
            0.1
HEALTHY ──────────► SICK
    \              /
 0.01 \           / 0.2
       ▼         ▼
         DEAD
```

With only these 3 states and the 3 transition probabilities every year, the model is complete. Table 5A shows how many people will now be in each condition every year as a result of the calculations of the model. At the start, all 1,000 people are healthy. After one year 0.1 x 1,000 = 100 people have become ill and 0.01 x 1,000 = 10 people have died. This means that 1,000 – 100 – 10 = 890 people remain in the healthy state (see the arrow returning to the same state). After the second year, 10% of those 890 have become ill = 0.1 x 890 = 89. There are also 1% who die (= 890 x 0.01 = 8.9, rounded up to 9) → after 2 years 890 – 89 – 9 = 792 remain in the healthy state.

The evolution of the state 'sick' is slightly more complex. After 1 year we had 100 sick people; after 2 years, 20 of the 100 sick people have died (0.2 x 100 =20) so that 80 remain. In addition to those 80 there are still the 89 people who were healthy in the previous year → the total is now 80 + 89 =169.
Finally, after one year, 10 people had died. After two years there are another 9 (from the 'healthy' state) and 20 (from the 'sick' state) who die. The total is now 10 + 29 = 39. In the same way, it is found that after three years, 705, 214 and 81 people are in the states 'healthy', 'sick' and 'dead' respectively.

A Markov model is useful in order to describe (or better: predict) the long term evolution of chronic diseases when data are only available for a limited period. In a health economic evaluation, this evolution is described twice: once with strategy A and once with strategy B. In the simple example given above, it is possible to conceive a treatment which will reduce the probability of evolving from 'healthy' to 'sick' to 0.05 (the original value was 0.1). This means that the evolution becomes as indicated in Table 5B. It should be noted that influencing

Table 5:   Result of a simple Markov model

A: on the basis of the figures in Figure 17

	At the start	After 1 year	After 2 years	After 3 years
Healthy	1000	890	792	705
Sick	0	100	169	214
Dead	0	10	39	81
Total	**1000**	**1000**	**1000**	**1000**

B: after adjusting the probability 'healthy' → 'sick' from 0.1 to 0.05.

	At the start	After 1 year	After 2 years	After 3 years
Healthy	1000	940	884	831
Sick	0	50	87	114
Dead	0	10	29	56
Total	**1000**	**1000**	**1000**	**1000**

C: after adjusting the probability 'sick' → 'dead' from 0.2 to 0.1

	At the start	After 1 year	After 2 years	After 3 years
Healthy	1000	890	792	705
Sick	0	100	179	240
Dead	0	10	29	55
Total	**1000**	**1000**	**1000**	**1000**

the chance of becoming ill also reduces the number of deaths. This is a strong point of Markov models: it is not necessary to set up long-term clinical studies to show an effect on mortality, if it is known that this effect can be achieved by having an effect on an intermediary result (here 'sick'). Obviously this is only possible when the link between the conditions 'sick' and 'dead' have already been demonstrated. Often, such a link is not well documented, which makes the prediction of the Markov model much less reliable.

In the last example (part C of the table) we simulate the result of reducing the chance of evolving from sick to dead from 0.2 to 0.1. This achieves the same effect on mortality, but at any one time more people are ill than in the second example (part B). This appears to indicate that an intervention closer to the start of the Markov chain

3.5 A real example of a Markov model: the treatment of breast cancer

The following example was inspired by a model proposed by Cocquyt et al. [42] and Moeremans et al. [43] in the field of breast cancer. Following the treatment of the primary cancer, a patient may find herself in one of the following states.

1. No further progression: the patient is still in a 'progression-free' condition, i.e. without relapse;
2. Local relapse: the patient has a relapse but this relapse is local (no metastasis);
3. Metastasis;
4. Death.

There are 4 possible states. At the start of the model every patient is in state 1. Suppose now that the fixed period (cycle) is defined as 6 months, and that 20 cycles are considered. This means that the total duration of the model is 10 years (20 x 6 months = 10 years). Table 6 below (known as a *transition matrix*), shows the transition probabilities among the different states.

It should be noted that the sum of all the transition probabilities from a particular state is equal to 1. For example, when someone is in state 2 (local relapse) at the beginning of a cycle, the chance of being in state 3 (metastasis) at the end of the cycle (6 months later) is equal to 10%, and the chance of being in state 4 is equal to 1%. The remaining 89% remains in state 2. It should also be noted that every period can have a different transition matrix since the probability of evolv-

---

[42] Cocquyt V, Moeremans K, Annemans L, Clarys P, Van Belle S. Long-term medical costs of postmenopausal breast cancer therapy. Ann Oncol. 2003 Jul;14(7):1057-63.

[43] Moeremans K, Annemans L. Cost-effectiveness of anastrozole compared to tamoxifen in hormone receptor-positive early breast cancer. Analysis based on the ATAC trial. Int J Gynecol Cancer. 2006;16 Suppl 2:576-8.

ing from a particular state to another state can vary over time. Examples of such variation can be found in the literature, but it is not the case in our example here.

Table 6: Data input for the Markov model in breast cancer

Strategy A

State at the end of every cycle → State at the start of every cycle ↓	State 1	State 2	State 3	State 4	Total
State 1	0.95	0.01	0.03	0.01	1
State 2	-	0.89	0.1	0.01	1
State 3	-	-	0.8	0.2	1
State 4	0	0	0	1	1

Strategy B

State at the end of every cycle → State at the start of every cycle ↓	State 1	State 2	State 3	State 4	Total
State 1	0.97	0.005	0.015	0.01	1
State 2	-	0.89	0.1	0.01	1
State 3	-	-	0.8	0.2	1
State 4	0	0	0	1	1

State 1: No further progression: the patient is still in a condition without a relapse;
State 2: Local relapse: the patient has a relapse but this relapse is local (no metastasis);
State 3: Metastasis;
State 4: Death.
Example: Strategy A: among those who are at the start of a cycle in state 2, 89% will remain in state 2 at the end of the cycle, 10% will have progressed to state 3 and 1% will have died.

Given, then, that in this example the probabilities are constant, the evolution of a cohort of patients can be predicted by applying these transitions 20 times (i.e. during 20 consecutive cycles). This is done as follows for strategy A:

We start with a virtual cohort of 10,000 patients (it could also be 1,000, or 100, or even 1 average virtual patient; this size of the cohort can be determined by the researcher).

After 6 months
- there are already 100 patients in state 2 (1% of 10,000);
- there are already 300 patients in state 3 (3% of 10,000);
- 100 patients have already died (state 4) (1% of 10,000);
- there are still 9,500 patients in state 1 (the remainder).

After 12 months
- there are 184 patients in state 2 as a result of 95 patients who have evolved from state 1 to state 2 (1% of 9,500) and 11 who have disappeared (10% of the 100 who were there are now in the metastasis state and 1% have died): 100 - 11 + 95 = 184
- there are 535 patients in state 3 (as a result of patients leaving and entering this state);
- 256 patients have died (state 4) by now;
- there are still 9,025 patients in state 1.

And so on and so on…

Figure 18 shows the evolution over 20 periods for *'one average patient'*. The solid lines show the evolution for the current strategy A. The X-axis shows the 20 periods (cycles); the Y axis shows the probability of being in a certain state at any time. Table 7 shows the same calculation to 4 decimal points. To determine how many patients are at each time in each of the states, the figures in the table must simply be multiplied by the cohort size (here 10,000). For instance, as explained above, when starting with 10,000 patients, after one cycle 9,500 among them will still be in the state 'no progression' with strategy A.

Imagine that the new intervention B reduces the chances of evolving from the first state to a local relapse or to metastasis by 50% in relative terms. The chance of evolving to a relapse is therefore 0.005 (50% of 0.01), and the chance of evolving to metastasis is therefore 0.015 (50% of 0.03; see Table 6). (The probabilities of evolving from relapse to metastasis and for evolving from metastasis to death remain unchanged.) Because of this reduction in these two transition probabilities, the evolution of the cohort looks obviously different, as shown by the dotted lines in Figure 18; see also the right-hand side of Table 7.

When starting with 10,000 patients, after one cycle 9,700 among them will still be in the state 'no progression' with strategy B.

Figure 18: Result of the Markov model. The solid lines show the evolution for strategy A, the dotted lines for strategy B.

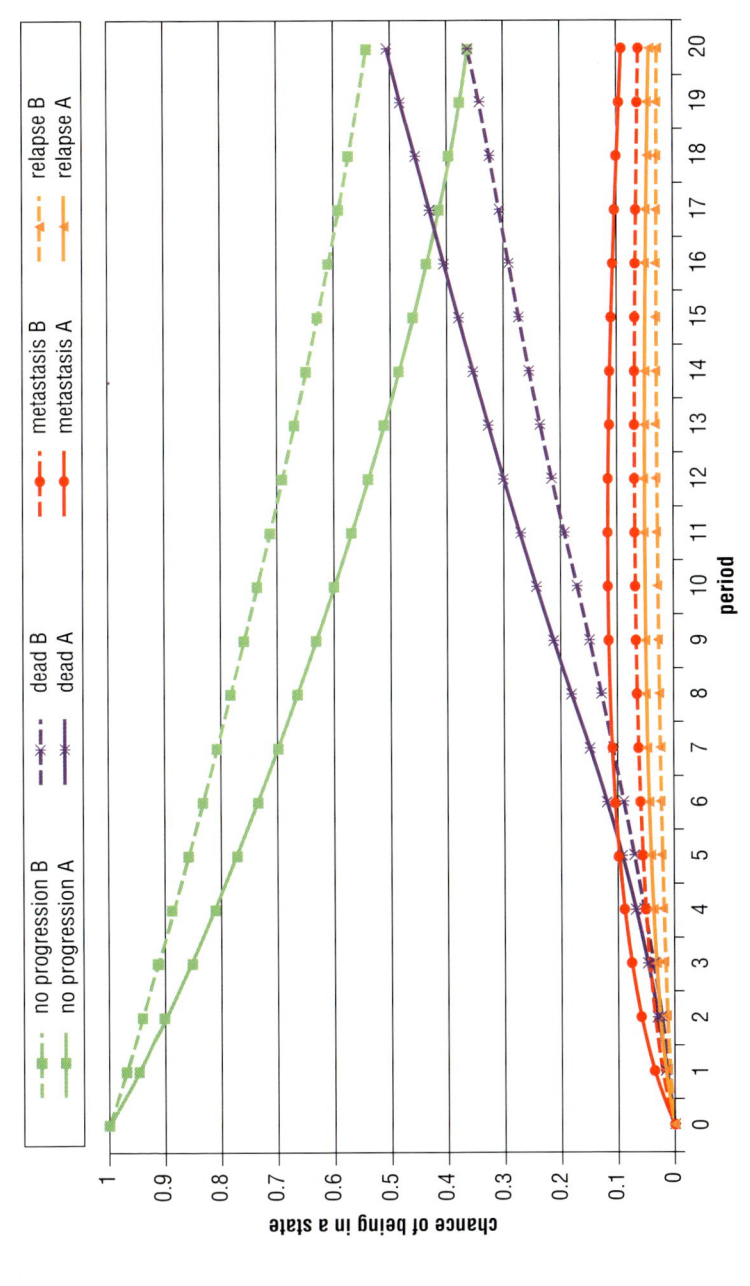

Table 7: Result of the calculation of the Markov model with strategy A and strategy B, for one average patient.

Period*	no progr A	relapse A	meta A	dead A	total	no progr B	relapse B	meta B	dead B	total
0 (start)	1.0000	0.0000	0.0000	0.0000	1.0	1.0000	0.0000	0.0000	0.0000	1.0
1	0.9500	0.0100	0.0300	0.0100	1.0	0.9700	0.0050	0.0150	0.0100	1.0
2	0.9025	0.0184	0.0535	0.0256	1.0	0.9409	0.0093	0.0271	0.0228	1.0
3	0.8574	0.0254	0.0717	0.0455	1.0	0.9127	0.0130	0.0367	0.0377	1.0
4	0.8145	0.0312	0.0856	0.0687	1.0	0.8853	0.0161	0.0443	0.0543	1.0
5	0.7738	0.0359	0.0961	0.0943	1.0	0.8587	0.0188	0.0504	0.0721	1.0
6	0.7351	0.0397	0.1037	0.1216	1.0	0.8330	0.0210	0.0550	0.0910	1.0
7	0.6983	0.0427	0.1089	0.1501	1.0	0.8080	0.0229	0.0586	0.1105	1.0
8	0.6634	0.0450	0.1124	0.1792	1.0	0.7837	0.0244	0.0613	0.1306	1.0
9	0.6302	0.0466	0.1143	0.2088	1.0	0.7602	0.0256	0.0632	0.1509	1.0
10	0.5987	0.0478	0.1150	0.2384	1.0	0.7374	0.0266	0.0646	0.1714	1.0
11	0.5688	0.0485	0.1148	0.2679	1.0	0.7153	0.0274	0.0654	0.1920	1.0
12	0.5404	0.0489	0.1137	0.2970	1.0	0.6938	0.0279	0.0658	0.2125	1.0
13	0.5133	0.0489	0.1121	0.3257	1.0	0.6730	0.0283	0.0658	0.2328	1.0
14	0.4877	0.0487	0.1100	0.3537	1.0	0.6528	0.0286	0.0656	0.2530	1.0
15	0.4633	0.0482	0.1075	0.3811	1.0	0.6333	0.0287	0.0651	0.2729	1.0
16	0.4401	0.0475	0.1047	0.4077	1.0	0.6143	0.0287	0.0645	0.2926	1.0
17	0.4181	0.0467	0.1017	0.4335	1.0	0.5958	0.0286	0.0636	0.3119	1.0
18	0.3972	0.0457	0.0986	0.4585	1.0	0.5780	0.0285	0.0627	0.3309	1.0
19	0.3774	0.0447	0.0954	0.4826	1.0	0.5606	0.0282	0.0617	0.3495	1.0
20	0.3585	0.0435	0.0921	0.5059	1.0	0.5438	0.0279	0.0606	0.3677	1.0

* N.B: Period '1' means the end of the first cycle.

We are halfway through the story now. In the context of a health economic evaluation, we need two additional types of data: the cost of each state and the utility level for each (the level between 0 and 1 on the basis of which the QALYs can be calculated). Both are shown in Table 8. (Again, these figures can come from different sources, such as the literature or the researcher's own original studies.)

Table 8: Cost and utility per state in the Markov model for breast cancer.

	Cost per 6 months	Utility level
State 1	€1000	0.8
State 2	€5000	0.65
State 3	€20000	0.5
State 4	0	0

State 1: No further progression: the patient is still in a condition without relapse;
State 2: Local relapse: the patient has a relapse but this relapse is local (no metastasis);
State 3: Metastasis;
State 4: Death.

We can now calculate step by step the costs over time. We do this for an average patient who would have been treated either with treatment A or with treatment B.

Current treatment A

After 1 period, the chances of being in states 1, 2 and 3 are 0.950, 0.010 and 0.030 respectively (see Table 7, line 1). The *weighted cost* in the first 6 months is therefore
€1,000 x 0.9500 + €5,000 x 0.0100 + €20,000 x 0.0300 = €1,600

As in a decision tree, the average patient has a weighted cost, based on the probabilities and costs of the respective possible conditions. The only difference from a decision tree is that this calculation is now repeated every cycle.

The second six months leads to a cost of
€1,000 x 0.9025 + €5,000 x 0.0184 + €20,000 x 0.0535= €2,064.5

After one year the total cumulative cost is €1,600 + €2,064.5 = €3,664.5

This process is continued over all cycles.

<u>New treatment B (with 50% reduction of the chances of a relapse and metastasis)</u>

After 1 period the chances of being in states 1, 2 and 3 are 0.9700, 0.0050 and 0.0150 respectively (see Table 7, line 1, right-hand side).

The weighted cost in the first 6 months is therefore
€1,000 x 0.9700 + €5,000 x 0.0050 + €20,000 x 0.0150 = €1,295

The second 6 months results in costs of
€1,000 x 0.9409 + €5,000 x 0.0093 + €20,000 x 0.0271= €1,528.4

After 1 year, the total cost is €1,295 + €1,528.4 = €2,823.4

This process is again continued over all cycles;

In this way, the model calculates the weighted cost for every period of 6 months and then the cumulative cost for 20 periods of 6 months (=10 years), for both strategies.

For the calculation of QALYs, the same approach is adopted, but not forgetting that 1 QALY is 1 Quality adjusted Life *Year*. A patient who is in a state with a utility value of 0.8 for 1 year has 0.8 QALYs; a patient who is in a state with a utility value of 0.8 for *half a year* has 0.8 x 0.5 = 0.4 QALYs.

Let's try it:

<u>Current treatment A</u>

After 1 period, the chance of being in states 1, 2 and 3 are 0.950, 0.010 and 0.030 respectively (see Table 7, line 1).
The weighted number of QALYs (see QALY values in Table 8) in the first six months is therefore:
(0.8×0.5) x 0.950 + (0.65×0.5) x 0.010 + (0.5×0.5) x 0.030 = 0.3908

In the second 6 months the number of QALYs is:
(0.8×0.5) x 0.9025 + (0.65×0.5) x 0.0184 + (0.5×0.5) x 0.0535 = 0.3804

After one year the cumulative number of QALYs is already 0.3908 + 0.3804 = 0.7712.
(note that the theoretical maximum after 1 year is 1; i.e. living for one year in full health).

New treatment B (with 50% reduction of the chances of a relapse and metastasis).

After 1 period, the chances of being in states 1, 2 and 3 are 0.9700, 0.0050 and 0.0150 respectively (see Table 7, line 1, right-hand side). Therefore the weighted number of QALYs in the first 6 months is

$(0.8 \times 0.5) \times 0.9700 + (0.65 \times 0.5) \times 0.0050 + (0.5 \times 0.5) \times 0.0150 = 0.3934$.

In the second cycle of 6 months the number of QALYs is

$(0.8 \times 0.5) \times 0.9409 + (0.65 \times 0.5) \times 0.0093 + (0.5 \times 0.5) \times 0.0271 = 0.3861$.

After one year, the cumulative number of QALYs is already 0.3934 + 0.3861 = 0.7795.

Once again, the cumulative result must be calculated for 20 periods of 6 months = 10 years.

The results for the total cost and for the total number of QALYs for both strategies is shown in Table 9.

With B we save, over a period of 10 years, €55,090 − €39,416 = €15,674, and we gain 6.3307 − 5.6255 = 0.7052 QALYs (see Table 9, line 20).

Table 9: Result of the Markov model in breast cancer

Cycle	A				B			
	Cost per cycle	Cumulative cost	QALY per cycle	Cumulative QALY	Cost per cycle	Cumulative cost	QALY per cycle	Cumulative QALY
0	0	0	0	0	0	0	0	0
1	1600	1600	0.3908	0.3908	1295	1295	0.3934	0.3934
2	2065	3665	0.3804	0.7712	1528	2823	0.3861	0.7795
3	2419	6083	0.3691	1.1402	1711	4535	0.3785	1.1580
4	2683	8766	0.3573	1.4976	1853	6387	0.3704	1.5284
5	2874	11641	0.3452	1.8428	1960	8347	0.3622	1.8906
6	3007	14647	0.3328	2.1756	2039	10386	0.3538	2.2444
7	3091	17738	0.3204	2.4961	2095	12481	0.3453	2.5897
8	3136	20873	0.3081	2.8041	2132	14613	0.3367	2.9264
9	3149	24023	0.2958	3.1000	2153	16766	0.3282	3.2546
10	3138	27161	0.2838	3.3838	2162	18927	0.3198	3.5744
11	3107	30267	0.2720	3.6557	2159	21087	0.3114	3.8857
12	3059	33327	0.2605	3.9162	2149	23236	0.3031	4.1888
13	2999	36326	0.2493	4.1655	2131	25366	0.2949	4.4837
14	2930	39256	0.2384	4.4038	2107	27474	0.2868	4.7705
15	2853	42110	0.2278	4.6317	2079	29552	0.2789	5.0494
16	2771	44881	0.2177	4.8494	2047	31599	0.2711	5.3205
17	2686	47567	0.2079	5.0572	2012	33611	0.2635	5.5841
18	2597	50164	0.1984	5.2556	1975	35586	0.2561	5.8402
19	2508	52672	0.1893	5.4449	1935	37521	0.2488	6.0890
20	2418	**55090**	0.1806	**5.6255**	1895	**39416**	0.2417	**6.3307**

Of course, we have not yet included in the above the cost of the therapy itself. Suppose therapy B costs €20,000 more than A (purchasing cost), then this extra cost of investing in B must be taken into account in the numerator of the ICER. The ICER becomes:

((**€20,000** + €39,416) - €55,090) / (6.3307-5.6255) = €4,326 / 0.7052 = €6134 per QALY.

If a threshold of around €30000/QALY is applied (see earlier), this seems to be a cost-effective result.

3.6 The validity of health economic models

To conclude these sections on decision models, it can be stated that they permit an extrapolation from often short-term clinical results to longer-term health economic results. They also make it possible to combine data from different sources in one decision-making framework.

Nevertheless, it is important that reports based on such models be read with a critical eye. Increasingly there is a demand for these sorts of models to be *validated*. With regard to the desirability of validation, a distinction may be made between different types. These are outlined below.

1. Structure validation: it is important to assure that the framework that has been created is a good representation of the real situation. In our model in the field of DVT, we did not make a distinction, for example, between proximal and distal DVT (for reasons of simplicity, keeping the didactic purpose in mind). However, the consequences of these two types of DVT are very different. Therefore a question arises with regard to the correct representation of reality. It should be noted that Haentjens et al. did indeed make this distinction (and actually found results which were different from those of our simplified example).

2. Content (or technical) validation: ideally, an expert reviewer should have the chance to examine the data input and model calculations. In the example in the field of breast cancer, it was explained that the processes taking place over 2 cycles were replicated exactly in the rest of the model and the result after 10 years

was made available immediately in Table 9. It is advisable to accept this kind of explanation only when there is a guarantee that it has been checked by a peer reviewer and that the data input, sources and calculations have been verified. This can be facilitated by providing the peer reviewer and even the end user with an electronic version of the model.

3. <u>Outcomes validation:</u> the model in the field of breast cancer calculates for the present strategy that after 10 years, 50.59% of the cohort will already have died (see previous section, Figure 18 and Table 7). If statistical data are available on actual mortality, it becomes possible to compare the prognosis of the model with reality. The closer the model approaches reality, the greater the validity of the results. (Obviously such validity cannot be assessed for the new treatment.)

4. <u>Assessment of robustness</u>: on the basis of *sensitivity analyses*, the extent to which the results of the model are sensitive to changes in the input data can be examined. This is discussed in the next section.

3.7 Sensitivity analysis

Suppose that in the model with regard to the prevention of DVT, the probability of a DVT with the strategy 'prolonged prophylaxis' is not 20% (as was originally the case – see Table 2) but 25%. Or suppose that it is actually lower, namely 15%. What are the consequences of this for the final result? The answer to this is usually shown in the following way (Figure 19):

Figure 19: Example of a sensitivity analysis in the DVT model – modified variable = probability of DVT with prolonged prophylaxis.

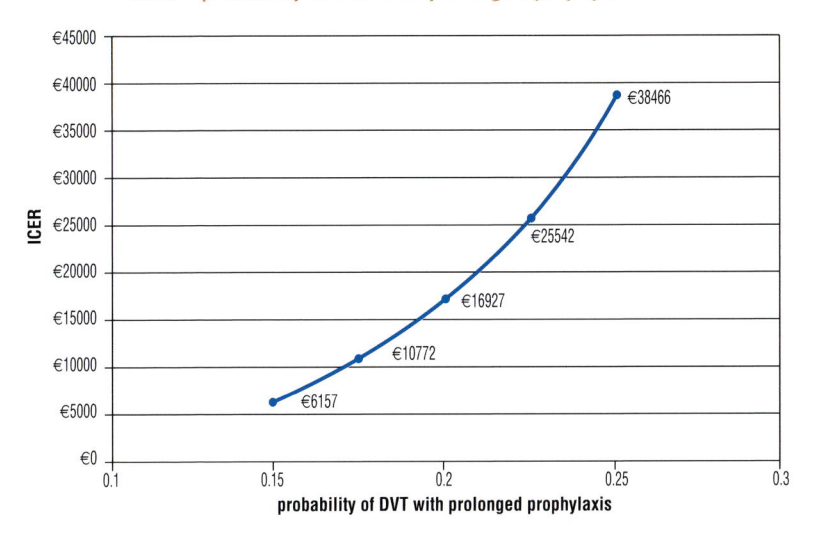

In this analysis, the model is calculated several times, each time with a different value for the chosen input variable. Note that the original result (also called the basecase result), namely €16,927/QALY, which corresponded to a probability of DVT of 20%, is found in the middle of the graph. We can now see from the graph that if this probability of a DVT with prolonged prophylaxis were to be 25% (which is of course a worse input), the ICER increases (deteriorates) to €38,466! Therefore it can be concluded that this model is very sensitive to a change in the probability of DVT.

Such a *one way sensitivity analysis* can be carried out for any input variable in the model. Figure 20, for instance, indicates how an increase or decrease in the cost of a PE influences the final result. With a decrease of €1,000, all the scenarios in the model which also contain a PE become €1,000 cheaper. The model is then calculated again leading to a new result. The model is also calculated again with a cost of PE which is €1,000 higher. Obviously, the higher the cost of PE, the more cost-effective the prophylaxis, because now a more expensive complication can be avoided.

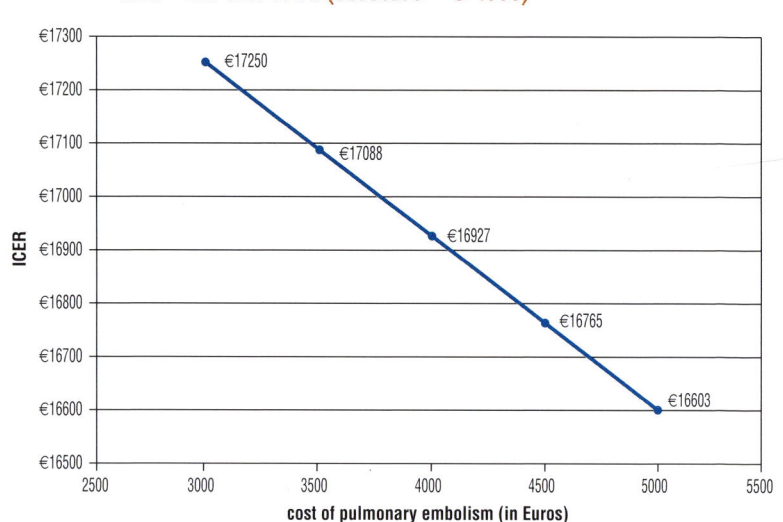

Figure 20: Example of a sensitivity analysis in the DVT model – modified variable = the cost of PE (basecase = € 4000)

(Graph showing ICER vs cost of pulmonary embolism (in Euros). Data points: (3000, €17250), (3500, €17088), (4000, €16927), (4500, €16765), (5000, €16603).)

Finally, I show an example of a sensitivity analysis for the breast cancer model. The result in section 3.5 is based on a time horizon of 10 years; that is, the costs and the QALYs were simulated for a period of 10 years. However, if a time horizon of only 5 years were taken, the result (see Table 9 with the cumulative results – line 10) would be very different indeed:

((€20,000 + €18,927) – €27,161)/ (3.5744 - 3.3838) = € 11,767 / 0.1906 = €61,725 per QALY.

This breast cancer model thus appears to be very sensitive to the time horizon of the analysis. A policy maker who prefers to make decisions based on short term data could therefore be less interested in the new strategy B for the treatment of breast cancer. (I come back to the aspect of time horizon in the section on guidelines - see below).

The above examples are so-called *one way* sensitivity analyses because only one input variable is changed. It is also possible to carry out 2-way analyses, in which 2 variables are simultaneously subjected to a change, or even multi-way analyses involving several variables. Figure 21 shows a 2-way sensitivity analysis, whereby (for reasons of simplicity) only the costs are considered as the model result. The 2 variables concerned are the probability of DVT with prolonged prophylaxis (in the basecase model = 0.20) and the cost of prolonged prophylaxis (in the basecase model = €130).

The green zone indicates for what combinations prolonged prophylaxis results in net savings. For example, if the probability of DVT with prolonged prophylaxis is 0.15, and the cost of that prolonged prophylaxis is only €80, then the prolonged prophylaxis strategy results in net savings (the figure does not show how much net savings, however). The orange zone shows the combinations for which prolonged prophylaxis is more expensive (again without showing the actual values). This sort of sensitivity analysis allows for a better, but rather qualitative, examination of the different scenarios.

Figure 21: Example of a 2-way sensitivity analysis in the DVT model – modified variables – chance of DVT with prolonged prophylaxis and cost of prolonged prophylaxis.

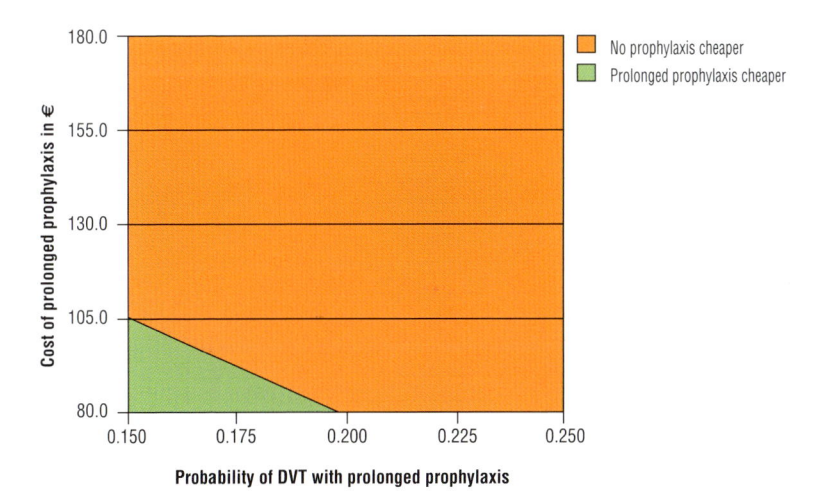

It is also possible to test 'worst case' scenarios, in which different variables assume an extreme but still feasible value which is to the disadvantage of the new treatment, and conversely, best-case scenarios.

The last type of sensitivity analysis is probabilistic sensitivity analysis (PSA), also sometimes known as a *Monte Carlo* analysis. This sort of analysis assumes that every input variable in the model is subject to uncertainty, characterized by a probability distribution. In this case, the probability of DVT with prolonged prophylaxis is not expressed as '0.20' (a deterministic value), but rather, for example, as a "normal distribution with an average of 0.20 and standard error of 0.05".

Below is a concrete calculation for a simple decision-making tree. It makes use of Figure 12 which is repeated here (as Figure 22).

Figure 22: Example of a decision tree with the calculation of expected costs and effects

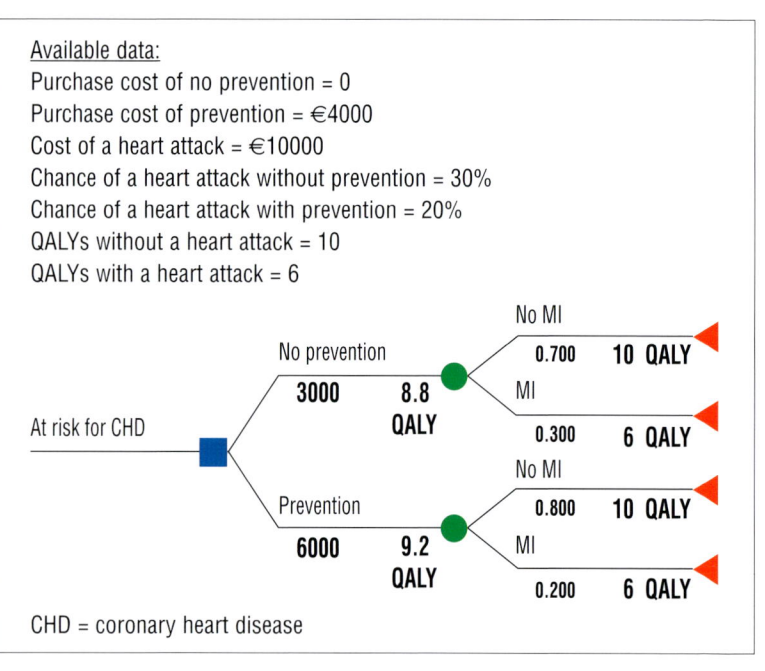

Available data:
Purchase cost of no prevention = 0
Purchase cost of prevention = €4000
Cost of a heart attack = €10000
Chance of a heart attack without prevention = 30%
Chance of a heart attack with prevention = 20%
QALYs without a heart attack = 10
QALYs with a heart attack = 6

```
                                         No MI
                   No prevention          0.700    10 QALY
                    3000      8.8
                              QALY        MI
At risk for CHD                           0.300    6 QALY
                                         No MI
                   Prevention             0.800    10 QALY
                    6000      9.2
                              QALY        MI
                                          0.200    6 QALY
```

CHD = coronary heart disease

The ICER for prevention compared with no prevention in this model was €7,500 per QALY. The calculation was (€6,000-€3,000) / (9.2 – 8.8) = €3,000 / 0.4 = €7,500/QALY (This is a good test to see whether you have remembered the principles.)

We will now subject a number of variables to a probability distribution.

- Suppose the cost of prevention is not €4,000 as was originally the case, but a normal distribution with average = €4,000 and standard error = €500.
- The cost of a heart attack is not €10,000, but a normal distribution with average = €10,000 and standard error = €1,000.
- The number of QALYs if there is no heart attack is not 10, but a

normal distribution with an average of 10 and a standard error of 1.
- The number of QALYs in case of a heart attack is not 6, but a normal distribution with an average of 6 and a standard error of 1.

We let the computer now calculate the model 500 times (many researchers use 1,000, or even 5,000 or 10,000 calculations). *Importantly, for every new calculation, the computer does not take exactly the average for the 4 above-mentioned variables, but a value chosen at random from their respective probability distributions.* When the model is calculated for the first time, for example, the computer might use:

Cost of prevention = €3,790 (and not €4,000)
Cost of a heart attack = €8,530 (and not €10,000)
Number of QALYs without MI = 10.5 (and not 10)
Number of QALYs with MI = 6.2 (and not 6).

With these inputs, the model leads to an ICER of €6,712 per QALY, as represented in Table 10. The results in Table 10 are again based on the concept of weighted average: e.g. Cost of No prevention = 0.7 x €0 + 0.3 x (€0 + €8,530) = €2,559
Cost of Prevention = 0.8 x €3,790 + 0.2 x (€3,790 +€8,530) = €5,496

Table 10: Result of one simulation in a probabilistic sensitivity analysis

Strategy	Cost (Euro)	Incremental Cost	Effect (QALY)	Incremental Effect	ICER (€/QALY)
No prevention	2559		9.2195		
Prevention	5496	2937	9.6571	0.4376	6712

In the second simulation, the input figures are again chosen randomly from the same respective probability distributions and we find an ICER of, for example, €4,060 per QALY. This procedure is repeated 500 times.

Figure 23 gives the result for these 500 repetitions. Every point in the figure represents the result of one calculation of the model. The green point is the average found earlier (0.4 extra QALYs at an extra cost of €3,000). The purple line shows a possible threshold for societal willingness to pay (in this example €20,000 per QALY). The majority of the points are below this threshold which suggests that the results of the model are robust.

It should be noted that in this example only 4 variables were subjected to a probability distribution. Ideally, as many variables as possible in the model should be characterised by this sort of probability distribution. It should also be noted that in the example we are working with normal distributions. In reality the distribution that is chosen must be the distribution which is most suitable for the type of variable.

For example, probabilities cannot be larger than 1 and cannot be smaller than 0. Therefore a normal distribution is not recommended and other distributions, such as binomial distributions or beta distributions are used. Cost inputs are often distributed in a non-normal way as well, and distributions such as the gamma distribution will often be used here. It would lead us too far to discuss this here. A reader who is interested in more of these mathematical and statistical details is referred to Claxton et al. (2005).[44]

Figure 23: Result of a probabilistic sensitivity analysis (Monte Carlo analysis)

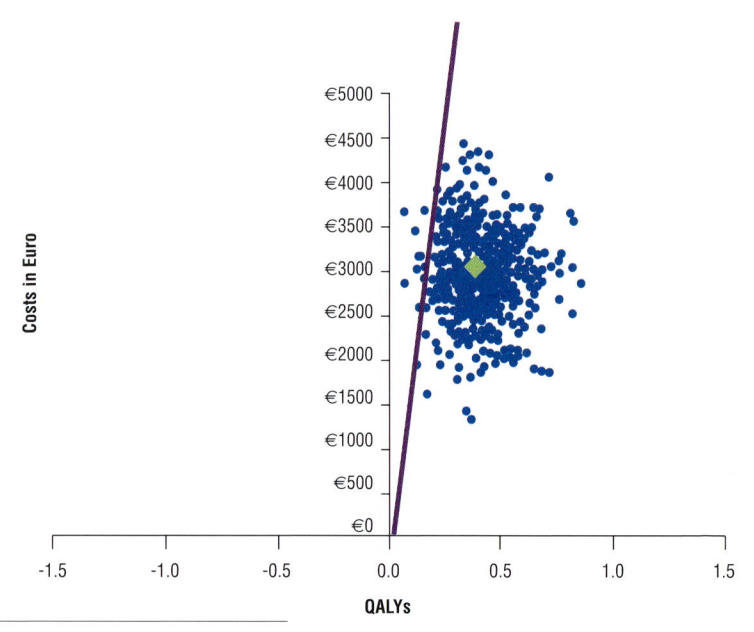

[44] Claxton K, et al. Probabilistic sensitivity analysis for NICE technology assessment: not an optional extra. Health Econ. 2005 Apr;14(4):339-47.

In addition to the presentation as in Figure 23, the results of a probabilistic sensitivity analysis can be presented as a *cost-effectiveness acceptability curve* (CEAC).

In such a graph (Figure 24) the horizontal axis shows different levels of societal willingness to pay for one unit of health (e.g. one QALY). The vertical axis shows the probability that the result of a health economic evaluation will be below that level.

For instance, if societal willingness to pay for a QALY is €20,000, then the curve shows there is a very high probability that prevention will be considered cost-effective. The exact figure is 98%. In other words, 98% of the dots from the first figure (Figure 23) are below the €20,000 threshold, which corresponds to a 98% acceptability level on the Y axis of Figure 24. The attractiveness of the acceptability curve is that the acceptability for any societal threshold can be observed in a single figure. [45]

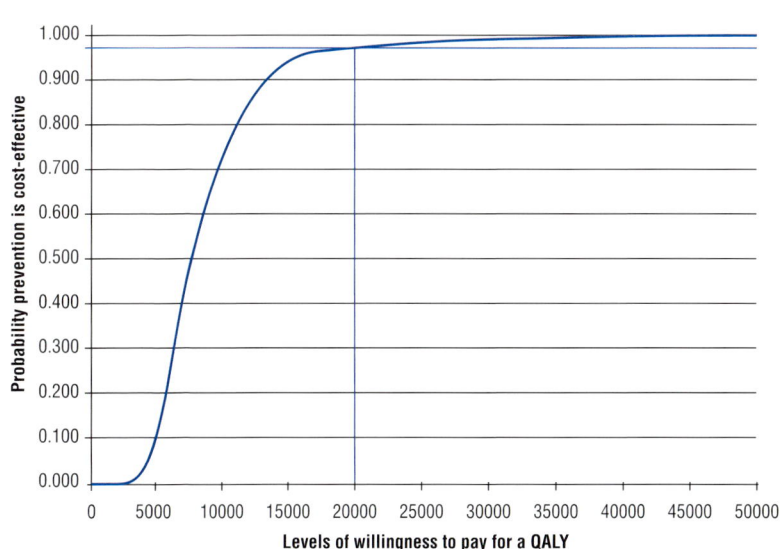

Figure 24: Cost-effectiveness acceptability curve

---

[45] Fenwick E, Claxton K, Sculpher M. Representing uncertainty: the role of cost-effectiveness acceptability curves. Health Econ. 2001 Dec;10(8):779-87.

3.8 Some examples of published health economic evaluations

In the last section of this chapter we return to some of the open questions which were raised in section 1.2:

- Are proton pump inhibitors cost-effective for patients with moderate reflux symptoms?
- For which women (of what age range) and with what frequency is it appropriate from the health economic point of view to screen for breast cancer?
- Do anti-depressants provide value for money as monotherapy or in combination with psychotherapy?
- Do cholesterol-lowering drugs provide value for money for patients who have only a moderately-increased cholesterol level but no other risk factors?

The answers shown below, based on published studies, reveal the ambiguities which can be involved. Please note that no systematic review has been conducted to formulate these answers. The aim is to make the reader more familiar with findings from the literature and how to interpret them. I have also opted to refer to the international literature as much as possible. What should certainly be clear is that more and better research is needed to reach stronger conclusions. Even in that case, it must be acknowledged that conclusions are only temporary because when there are new insights, or new technologies or medicines appear on the market, the situation will undoubtedly change.

- *Are proton pump inhibitors cost-effective for patients with moderate reflux symptoms?*

Gerson et al. (2000)[46] is one of the few studies in which a comparison is made between proton pump inhibitors (PPIs), H2 antagonists and lifestyle advice (the latter allowing for the use of antacids). This is an American study based on a decision model and data from meta-analyses. The authors come to the conclusion that the incremental cost-effectiveness of the pharmaceutical treatments for serious symptoms varies between $20,000 per QALY and $41,500 per QALY when compared to the 'lifestyle' strategy. For mild symptoms the incremental cost-effectiveness varies between $47,000 and $108,000 per QALY, which are quite high ratios. (The best pharmaceutical option is 'on demand' therapy with PPIs.) Hence, the study shows that starting medication immediately for mild reflux symptoms is not very cost-effective. The decision tree was, however, designed in such a way that following the failure of the first line lifestyle recommendations it was possible to start with the therapy. The correct interpretation is therefore important: "*starting with lifestyle advice is the most cost-effective way, but in the case of failure it is necessary to change to medication and subsequently – if there is further failure – to endoscopic examinations and possibly further interventions*".

- *For which women (of what age range) and with what frequency is it appropriate from a health economic point of view to screen for breast cancer?*

Various studies have shown that the impact of screening on mortality is strongest at an age between 50 and 70. The cost-effectiveness is not good for women of 40 because at that age the incidence of breast cancer is lower, so that many more women have to be screened to detect one case.[47] For age categories above approximately 70, the cost-effectiveness is poorer as well, this time because the advantages of screening are partly cancelled out by co-morbidities. In other words, the potential QALYs to be gained become smaller so that the denominator of the cost-effectiveness ratio decreases, and the cost-effectiveness ratio itself increases (and therefore becomes poorer).[48]

---

[46] Gerson L. et al. A Cost-Effectiveness Analysis of Prescribing Strategies in the Management of Gastroesophageal Reflux Disease. Am J Gastroenterol. 95, 2, 2000

[47] Salzmann P, et al. Cost-effectiveness of extending screening mammography guidelines to include women 40 to 49 years of age. Ann Intern Med. 1997 Dec 1;127(11):955-65.

[48] Mandelblatt J, et al. The cost-effectiveness of screening mammography beyond age 65 years: a systematic review for the U.S. Preventive Services Task Force. Ann Intern Med. 2003 Nov 18;139(10):835-42.

- *Do anti-depressants provide value for money as monotherapy or in combination with psychotherapy?*

Barrett et al. (2005)[49] indicate that there is little clarity in this field: too many scales, too many different study designs... leading to strongly divergent results. Nevertheless, their review allows us to conclude that SSRIs (selective serotonin receptor inhibitors) are admittedly more expensive than TCAs (tricyclical anti-depressants), but that the extra cost shows an acceptable ratio to the extra QALYs.

Kendrick et al. (2006)[50] studied the cost-effectiveness of SSRIs and TCAs in a prospective study over 12 months. The authors came to the conclusion that SSRIs are preferable if society is willing to pay £5,000 per QALY (which is often the case).

Pyne et al. (2005)[51] examined whether *any* treatment for depression with anti-depressants is actually cost-effective. Most studies compare drug A with drug B, but do not actually ask the question about the cost-effectiveness of anti-depressants as compared to 'doing nothing'. The authors come to the conclusion that for patients who are *receptive* to anti-depressants, a cost per QALY of $5,000 is achieved, while for patients who are not receptive, anti-depressants are not cost-effective at all. The authors recommend a better assessment of 'receptivity' before starting treatment.

A health economic evaluation by Simon et al. (2006)[52] in the UK comes to the conclusion, on the basis of a decision tree based on meta-analyses, that the cost per QALY of combination therapy compared with pharmacological therapy for serious depression is equal to £5,777 (95% confidence interval £1,900 - £33,800) per QALY. For moderate depression this cost-effectiveness is £14,540 (95% confidence interval £4,800 - £79,400) per QALY.

Finally, Chatwin et al. (2007)[53] describe the design of a study of the cost-effectiveness of anti-depressants for patients with mild to moderate depression. The authors indicate that little is known about this matter. At the time of writing, no results have yet emerged.

---

[49] Barrett B. et al Evidence of cost-effective treatments for depression: a systematic review. J Affect Disord. 2005; 84:1-13.

[50] Kendrick T, et al. Cost-effectiveness and cost-utility of tricyclic antidepressants, selective serotonin reuptake inhibitors and lofepramine: randomised controlled trial. Br J Psychiatry. 2006 Apr;188:337-45.

[51] Pyne JM, et al. One size fits some: the impact of patient treatment attitudes on the cost-effectiveness of a depression primary-care intervention. Psychol Med. 2005 Jun;35(6):839-54.

[52] Simon J, et al. Treatment options in moderate and severe depression: decision analysis supporting a clinical guideline. Br J Psychiatry. 2006 Dec;189:494-501.

[53] Chatwin J, Kendrick T; THREAD Study Group. Protocol for the THREAD (THREshold for AntiDepressants) study: a randomized controlled trial to determine the clinical and cost-effectiveness of antidepressants plus supportive care, versus supportive care alone, for mild to moderate depression in UK general practice. BMC Fam Pract. 2007 Jan 4;8:2.

What do these five examples from the field of depression tell us (without going into the methods in detail)? In the first place we find that it is not possible to generalise. Health economists nevertheless sometimes have a tendency to generalise, because most analyses work with averages. Given this tendency, the conclusions "SSRIs are cost-effective compared to TCAs" or "anti-depressants are cost-effective" are often reached. These conclusions are not very sensible. It is better to look for the subtype of patients for whom the conclusion does apply, by means of analysis and reanalysis if necessary. Not all depressive patients are receptive to anti-depressants, and when they are not, these products will not be cost-effective. In addition, it may be tempting to treat patients with mild symptoms but not a single indication of cost-effectiveness is available in this regard.

- *Do cholesterol-lowering drugs provide value for money for patients who only have moderately increased cholesterol levels, but no other risk factors?*

Currently it is generally accepted that cholesterol reducing drugs are cost-effective for 'secondary prevention' (for patients who already suffer from cardiovascular disease such as a myocardial infarction and stroke) and for very high-risk patients in primary prevention. [54] Johannesson (2001) [55] shows that it is only from a given risk level upwards that it is actually cost-effective to treat with statins in primary prevention. If society is prepared to pay a maximum of $40,000 per QALY, the level of the five-year risk of coronary heart disease must be at least 6.5% for a 50-year-old man and at least 21.36% for a 70-year-old man. For women the respective figures are 5.07% and 20.3%. Hence, only from a minimal risk level upwards does prevention become cost-effective.

It should also be noted that this study dates from 2001 and does not take into account the drop in the cost of statins since then. It does not take into account the differing efficacies of different statins either.

---

[54] De Backer G, et al. ESC. AHA. ACC. European guidelines on cardiovascular disease prevention in clinical practice. Third Joint Task Force of European and other Societies on Cardiovascular Disease Prevention in Clinical Practice. Atherosclerosis. 2004 Apr;173(2):381-91.

[55] Johannesson M. At what coronary risk level is it cost-effective to initiate cholesterol lowering drug treatment in primary prevention? European Heart Journal (2001) 22, 919–925.

4 Guidelines for conducting and assessing health economic evaluations

We now know what health economic evaluations are and how they are carried out. But by now it has probably also become clear that the results of these evaluations depend to a great extent on various methodological choices and assumptions. Changing one figure in a decision tree (the probability of success with a treatment, the time horizon of the model, the cost or the level of utility of a particular condition in a Markov model,...) can be enough to change the results. The choice of the therapies being compared can also lead to misleading conclusions: sometimes there is a deliberate comparison with an alternative which is already known to be either too expensive or has side effects, in order to produce a favourable result from the comparison. However, if this alternative is hardly used today, the comparison is obviously not relevant. In addition, information on the sources of input data is also sometimes rather vague, as is information about the way in which these figures are subsequently processed for use as input to the model.

For these reasons, when reading the results of a health economic evaluation, there are potential methodological problems round every corner. That is why guidelines have been developed. These guidelines can be very strict (so that if they are not followed, the evaluation is not considered to be of good quality and is rejected) or they can serve as a more general guide for carrying out evaluations. The first guidelines were developed in the early 1990s in Australia and Canada. In the mid and late 1990s many European countries followed. These guidelines are now due for review in the light of methodological developments. The International Society for Pharmacoeconomics and Outcomes Research (ISPOR) has not only taken the initiative to provide a summary of all existing international guidelines, but has also developed specific (non-binding) guidelines for particular types of research (e.g., guidelines for decision models, prospective health economic studies, retrospective health economic studies, ...). In this chapter, we discuss the most important guidelines. For these I have drawn on various published guidelines such as those issued by ISPOR [56] and more recently by those of the Belgian Knowledge Centre for Healthcare, which were in turn inspired by several international sets of guidelines. [57] In addition, we look at some important points with regard to specific methods which are insufficiently treated in the general guidelines.

4. Summary of the most important guidelines

10 recommendations which relate to the most important aspects of health economic research are discussed here.

4.1.1 The medical problem and the target population

It is first of all necessary to indicate clearly the medical problem and population of patients concerned. For example, if the medical problem is the occurrence of DVT in patients with major orthopaedic surgery (see section 3.3), the consequences of this problem must be clearly described (symptoms, chance of PE, chance of re-DVT, chance of PTS, etc.) so that the reader can judge whether the final analysis takes these different elements into account. The correct description of the target population is particularly important for subsequent population-wide extrapolations (ideally the authors should be able to indicate how many patients are eligible for this treatment in a given setting), but also for examining whether the input in the analysis, like the result of a clinical study, actually relates to the same patients as those described in the target population. Furthermore, it is also appropriate to show, as much as this is possible, the results for subpopulations of patients. For instance, it is better to have separate results for hip and for knee replacement patients in the target population of patients with 'major orthopaedic surgery'.

---

[56] www.ispor.org
[57] www.kce.fgov.be

4.1.2 Comparative therapies

The intervention that is examined must be compared with the most relevant alternative treatment for the target population and indication considered. This alternative is referred to as "the most likely to be replaced", in other words the therapy which has the greatest chance of being replaced by the intervention being examined. This requirement sometimes gives rise to problems because direct comparative clinical studies between the intervention examined and the relevant alternative are not always available. In that case methods of 'indirect comparison' must be applied, usually with meta-analyses. These fall outside the scope of this book, but the reader is referred to Hasselblad.[58] This guideline also includes the stipulation of a short, clear description of the intervention that is examined and its alternative, with their advantages and disadvantages.

On the basis of guidelines 1 and 2, the *aim* of the evaluation should now be clear. For example:

- "to examine the cost-effectiveness of prolonged prophylaxis with low molecular weight heparins after a total hip or knee replacement, compared to a short-term prophylaxis (up to discharge of the patient)", or
- "to examine the cost-effectiveness of anastrozole compared to tamoxifen, in the treatment of patients with primary breast cancer."

4.1.3 The perspective of the evaluation

Researchers must clearly indicate the perspective of their study. When a societal perspective is taken, this means that it is not only the costs and savings in the health sector that are taken into account, but also the economic consequences of lost productivity as a result of sickness. Several policy makers prefer a limited healthcare perspective, which is concerned only with direct medical costs (see section 2.2), because this is what their budget relates to. In fact, the societal perspective is preferred by many guidelines for health economic evaluations, but is less often applied in practice.

---

[58] Hasselblad V. Meta-analysis of multitreatment studies. Med Decis Making 1998;18:37–43.

If a hospital perspective is chosen, then only costs and savings from the perspective of the hospital manager are taken into account. For instance, if one can switch within the hospital setting from IV antibiotics to oral antibiotics, this means less nursing time and material, which means a potential saving for the hospital manager, but not necessarily a saving for the health insurer who pays a fixed fee ('charge') for the hospital stay.

4.1.4 Design of the study

Earlier in this book, we have seen the advantages and disadvantages of observational data collection and models. In many cases models will be needed because the observational data are inadequate to give a complete picture of all the costs and health effects by themselves. However, the input of these models must ideally be based at least on some (preferably observational) data in a comparative context between the intervention being examined and the alternative. Furthermore, assumptions in the model must be reduced to a minimum and must be reported transparently. It is increasingly recommended that an electronic copy of the model should be made available, together with the research report.

4.1.5 Calculating costs

Costs must always be examined and reported in 3 stages:
- the *identification* of costs (which costs are included in the calculations and which are not, and why);
- *measuring* the elements which cause these costs. These must be expressed in 'natural' units (e.g. number of consultations, number of hospital admissions, number of days in hospital), and sources must be shown and explained in a transparent manner;
- the *valorisation* of every unit.

This last step involves choosing the unit cost which best applies to the chosen perspective. For example, "from the perspective of health insurance, a consultation with a general practitioner costs €20.79" (this value can of course change over time). Note that we have seen that the true costs of such a consultation may be different from the 'charges'. But since the unit cost must fit the perspective, in the case of the health insurance this unit cost is indeed often the 'charge'.

4.1.6 Calculating health effects

In health economic evaluations we are interested in what is known as 'hard endpoints': fewer metastases, fewer heart attacks, fewer cases of depression, etc. The ultimate result according to several authors, and *if* one wants to make cross-disease comparisons, is the QALY, as shown above. This must be measured by assigning a utility weight to the different conditions in which patients can find themselves.

When improving the quality of life is the most important objective of the intervention, or when there are several clinical results of a different order and size, and even different directions (e.g., the new treatment is more effective but also has side effects), a cost per QALY analysis (described by some authors as a cost-utility analysis) is often the most appropriate, especially when the decision maker is interested in cross-disease comparisons. When extending life is the main aim, then it is possible to consider a cost per gained year of life. However, even then it should be pointed out that if life is extended by 6 months (= 0.5 years), and the patient has a quality of life weight of 0.2, only 0.5 x 0.2 = 0.1 QALY is gained (see also section 2.4.2). If the incremental cost of this treatment is €10,000, this means €20,000 (namely €10,000/0.5) for each year of life that is gained (which would seem more or less acceptable) but it means €100,000 (€10,000/0.1) for each QALY that is gained, which seems much less acceptable.

If the decision maker is not interested in QALYs and cross-disease comparisons, then a disease specific outcome (e.g. avoided major cardiovascular events, avoided relapse of cancer) can be used.

As is the case for costs, the sources used to collect the clinical input data (probabilities in the tree, utilities, etc.) must be represented in a transparent manner and explained.

4.1.7 Time horizon

The choice of the time horizon is one of the most difficult decisions in a health economic evaluation. It will depend to a large extent on the nature of the disease that is examined. It is certainly necessary to ensure that *all* the relevant costs and effects can be captured. Chronic progressive diseases and acute diseases with long-term consequences obviously require a long time horizon, sometimes even lifelong. However, following Cocquyt et al.[42], for our example of breast cancer a time horizon of only 10 years was used. The reason for not using a longer duration there was the lack of observational data in the longer term and therefore the impossibility of carrying out a validation of the outcomes (see above, section 3.6). With a ten-year prediction this 'outcomes validation' was possible, at least in the field of breast cancer, where observational data over such a time period existed. Even longer data are now available.[59] The choice of time horizon can therefore also depend on the availability of data. It is in any case possible to use relatively short time horizons for acute diseases without long-term consequences or complications.

It is increasingly recommended that an uncertainty analysis be carried out on the time horizon, in which it is asked: "what would be the result if the time horizon was only X years?". With regard to this, see the sensitivity analysis in section 3.7. above.

4.1.8 Uncertainty analysis

It is essential to carry out an uncertainty analysis for every study. One-way, two-way or multi-way sensitivity analyses are recommended, as well as a worst case and a best case scenario (see section 3.7.). Obviously the limits (lower limit and upper limit) of each sensitivity analysis must be realistic and based on observations or published sources. For example, it is not sufficient to vary all the input variables by 10% upwards or downwards when the data show that larger variations are possible. A common mistake is to subject only some variables to a sensitivity analysis, so that it is not possible for the reader to estimate the impact of the other variables.

Ideally a probabilistic sensitivity analysis (PSA) should also be carried out (see the example in section 3.7.). This has the advantage that all the uncertainties are examined *together*, and that in addition, the chance of a certain combination of variables occurring is known. In fact, a worst case scenario tells us what the worst possible results of

---

[42] Cocquyt V, Moeremans K, Annemans L, Clarys P, Van Belle S. Long-term medical costs of post-menopausal breast cancer therapy. Ann Oncol. 2003 Jul;14(7):1057-63.

[59] Early Breast Cancer Trialists' Collaborative Group (EBCTCG). Effects of chemotherapy and hormonal therapy for early breast cancer on recurrence and 15-year survival: an overview of the randomised trials. Lancet. 2005 May 14-20;365(9472):1687-717.

4.1.9 Discounting future amounts

One concept that has been absent from this book so far is *discounting*. It has been deliberately omitted until this point because it is a rather purely economic concept. It entails that future amounts must be calculated back to their present value. The reason for the need for discounting is that people have a time preference. We want short-term satisfaction and prefer to push costs away as far as possible. Discounting means actually giving a present value to future costs and effects, depending on the time at which they occur. One example with regard to costs: suppose that we vaccinate today (cost = €100) to save €100 ten years later. For example, this saving of €100 is the result of the conclusion that without the vaccination 1% of the population will catch the disease and that the disease itself costs €10,000. If the vaccine is fully effective and avoids the 1% incidence of the disease, we will save 1% of €10,000 = €100 with the vaccine (via the simple application of the concept of a decision tree).

However, the €100 saving will *not* have the same value after ten years as €100 has today. By way of comparison, if someone owes you the sum of €100 and simply states that he/she will give you that sum in ten years time from now, you will not appreciate it. €100 ten years from now will be worth less than €100 today. But how much will it be worth? This depends on the *discount rate* that is used. Suppose this discount rate is 3%, in that case it can be calculated that €100 ten years from now will have the same value as €74.4 today. This calculation is carried out as follows:

€100/(1 + 0.03) = €100/1.03 is the value after nine years
(€100/(1 + 0.03))/(1 + 0.03) is the value after eight years. This can also be written as €100/(1.03)^2.
Continuing the same argument, the value today will be €100/(1.03)^{10}
This value is known as the net present value of a future amount of money.

Every country adopts its own guidelines with regard to the discount rate that is to be used. For example, in many guidelines it is stated that future costs must be discounted at 3%.

Many health economists believe that future health effects must be discounted as well. According to their arguments, saving a life ten years from now does not have the same value as saving a life today. The discounting of effects may be explained by uncertainty. This uncertainty can arise because the effect may not be achieved or because this effect may be obtained or avoided in another way. For example, what does it mean to avoid cancer in twenty years' time? Perhaps there will be a new treatment by then.

There is less consensus with regard to discounting effects than there is with regard to discounting costs. Some authors believe it is not necessary at all, while others argue that it is necessary but to a lesser extent and that a lower discount rate should be adopted than that applied to costs. The latter would recommend, for instance, a 3% discount rate for costs and 1.5% for effects.

The level of the discount rate may have a strong impact on the final results of a health economic evaluation, especially if the timing of the costs and the effects are different. For example, if one vaccinates now against Hepatitis B in order to avoid liver cancer 25 years later, the discounting will have a great impact. Indeed, the future savings from avoiding liver cancer will be discounted and show a rather low present value. On the other hand, when statins are taken for thirty years in order to avoid cardiovascular risks, the costs (statins) and effects (avoided cardiovascular disease) are less far apart from each other. Another example: the costs and effects are almost entirely simultaneous in the case of kidney dialysis. When the dialysis stops, the effect (namely that the patient is kept alive) also disappears. In this last case, discounting will not have any impact on the end result (the ratio between costs and effects).

4.1.10 Conclusions and extrapolations

Every health economic evaluation must give rise to clear conclusions. Amongst other things this means that it is reported for what indications, what patients, and in comparison with what alternatives a certain cost-effectiveness value was found. It is not acceptable to state in general terms that a medicine or a technology is cost-effective. This conclusion must always be accompanied by the indication, the target population and the strategy with which comparisons were made. The conclusion must also indicate to what extent the results are robust (on the basis of the sensitivity analysis) and which variables should be subjected to further examination in the future. Finally, it is also recommended that the consequences of a decision on using a new medicine or technology should be represented at the level of the *whole population*.

Birch and Gafni (2006)[60] illustrate this last point using the example of a purchase of cornflakes. Suppose you want to buy cornflakes and you compare the different products regarding their cost per 100g (some supermarkets give this information). If you follow the rules of decision-making based on 'value for money', you would choose the product with the lowest cost per 100g (assuming they all have the same quality). However, suppose you can only buy that product in a packet of 100 *kilograms* (a slight exaggeration). In that case, you would certainly not opt for it because you do not have the budget for it. The same thing applies for medicines and technologies: a cost-effective result at the individual patient level can extrapolate to an immense budgetary impact at the population level, and this must at least be indicated to the policy maker. If no extra budgets are made available, the money must come from existing funds, and therefore other treatments will have to be sacrificed. I return to budgetary impact in the next chapter.

4.2 Specific guidelines for specific methods

The 10 recommendations of the previous section can serve the reader of a report or paper as a guideline for a rough assessment of the quality of a health economic evaluation, or for the researcher in the design of one. However, these recommendations are not sufficient. For example, they include no mention of the different types of validation of a model (see 3.6), or of how to deal with a selection bias in a retrospective study (see 3.1.1), or of looking at the external validity of a prospective study (see 3.1.2). Therefore it is also important to be aware of guidelines which pertain to a given method. Guidelines for modelling, retrospective studies and prospective studies are discussed in turn in the following subsections.

---

[60] Birch S, Gafni A. Information created to evade reality (ICER): things we should not look to for answers. Pharmacoeconomics. 2006;24(11):1121-31.

4.2.1 Guidelines for models

In 2003 Weinstein et al. developed guidelines focusing specifically on decision-making models and Markov analyses. [61] The most important additional elements (in relation to the general guidelines above) in these guidelines for models are as follows:

- Every model must undergo a validation process with respect to structure, content and outcomes (see section 3.6. above).

- In connection with structure validation, Weinstein et al. point out that the inputs and outputs must be relevant for the decision maker (the policy maker, payer or care provider), and that the structure of the model must be consistent with a coherent theory of the condition of the disease being examined and its consequences. Any relationship between variables shown in the model (e.g., "DVT leads to PE in 0.8% of cases") must not contradict current knowledge and must be consistent with current theories. The authors also emphasize that the model should be a representation of reality while remaining as simple as possible.
Finally, they also remind us that in a valid health economic evaluation, all the economic and clinical consequences of side effects must be included. For instance, it would perhaps have been better to include the extra risk of bleeding with extended use of heparins in the calculations in the decision tree for the prevention of DVT. After all, bleeding means extra costs and fewer QALYs.

- With regard to Markov models, if the chance of moving from a state 2 to a state 3 can be influenced by the prior history of the patient (was the patient ever in state 1, and if so, for how long?), this 'memory function' must be present in the model.

- The duration of one cycle in a Markov model (6 months in the breast cancer model) must be chosen in such a way that multiple transitions from and to a disease state are improbable within one and the same cycle. For example, if a local relapse as well as a metastasis often develops within 6 months in the same patient, it is better to shorten the length of the cycle.

---

[61] Weinstein MC, et al. ISPOR Task Force on Good Research Practices--Modeling Studies. Principles of good practice for decision analytic modeling in health-care evaluation: report of the ISPOR Task Force on Good Research Practices—Modeling Studies. Value Health. 2003 Jan-Feb;6(1):9-17.

- In connection with content validation, Weinstein et al assert that a systematic review must form the basis for the input of clinical data. This is logical because otherwise the builder of the model might be inclined to select those clinical data which have a positive influence on the results. On the other hand, a lack of data does not mean that it is not possible to make a model. The use of assumptions, as long as they are transparently represented and accompanied by possible alternatives and the necessary sensitivity analyses, is permitted because these give the policy maker and decision maker an insight into the dynamics of the model and the impact of various variables (and of the assumptions concerned) on the end result.

- For every input variable it is necessary not only to give an average value, but also an idea of the uncertainty around that average. Examples are: minimum-maximum figures; 5th percentile, 95th percentile; a confidence interval.

- Finally, all the mathematical relationships must be transparently reported.

Note that Weinstein et al use a different terminology for validation from that used in this book. They refer to *internal validation*, *inter-model validation*, and *external validation*. In this terminology, internal validation contains, amongst others, the following elements:

- A recalculation and checking for mistakes;
- The 'calibration' (i.e. the comparison of the model output - the current treatment - with observations from existing studies) and if necessary correction of the model in order to achieve a better correspondence with reality (we have called this 'outcomes validation');
- Making an electronic copy available in order to share the 'programming code' with others, particularly the end user.

Inter-model validity can be achieved by comparing different models of the same condition or disease. This is usually done in the discussion part of a report.

External validation relates to the extent to which it is possible to successfully adapt a model to new data and knowledge. It is important to understand that models should never be seen as being complete and unchangeable. Depending on new data and knowledge, they must be adapted, both in terms of structure and in terms of content. External validity also comprises so-called predictive validity, which is achieved by comparing the original results of the model with observational data which have been collected since the new medicine or technology became available.

4.2.2 Guidelines for retrospective studies

Motheral et al. (2003) [62] offer specific guidelines for retrospective designs for health economic evaluations. (By way of reminder: these studies look back and examine the health economic consequences of a treatment A and a treatment B over a particular period from the start of treatment.) The guidelines include, amongst other things:

- The correct description of which data are available and which data are not available in the retrospective data source.
- Information about the way in which the quality of the data was checked. As stated earlier in this book, retrospective data sometimes suffer from poor data collection quality. For example, if data are taken from patient files, the extent to which these files were originally completed correctly will determine the quality of the research.
- The exact description of the patients (inclusion and exclusion criteria) who are the subjects of the study. This requires more detail than the general description of the target population.
- An indication of the possible disadvantages of the chosen design. Remember, the best-known problem with a retrospective design is the *selection bias* referred to earlier.
- A representation of the period of time during which the data are available. Sometimes patients disappear from the study, for example because they change to another health care centre or because they die. Obviously the data analysis must take this 'censoring' of the data into account.
- The correct definition of endpoints. Suppose the endpoint is a DVT. How is this defined? Is it defined with an ICD-9 code (International Classification of Diseases), on the basis of reported symptoms in the patient file, on the basis of the use of intravenous heparin, or on some other basis? The choice of this definition will obviously influence the result.

---

[62] Motheral B, Brooks J, Clark MA, Crown WH, Davey P, Hutchins D, Martin BC, Stang P. A checklist for retrospective database studies--report of the ISPOR Task Force on Retrospective Databases. Value Health. 2003 Mar-Apr;6(2):90-7.

- The description of the relationship over time between the treatment options and the endpoint. For example, can a DVT which only occurs after three months still be associated with the initial treatment choice? For what length of time is this link presumed to exist?

4.2.3 Guidelines for prospective studies

Finally, specific guidelines have also been developed for prospective studies.[63] These guidelines pertain to the design, execution and reporting of cost-effectiveness analyses within the context of clinical studies.

According to the authors of these guidelines:

- more effort must be made to allow clinical studies to measure effectiveness rather than efficacy (see definitions in section 1.2).
- collecting the data on medical consumption must be fully integrated in the study and must take place on the basis of the medical consumption of each and every individual in the study. This makes it possible to determine averages and distributions.
- every study must be preceded by the formulation of a hypothesis and an analysis plan.
- it is essential that all the patients continue to be followed up, even when there is a negative outcome for a patient.
- all other threats to external validity (see section 3.1.1), such as protocol-driven medical consumption, non-representative participating centres (e.g. expert centres, whereas in the real world the patients involved are treated by their general practitioner), restrictive inclusion and exclusion criteria and artificially improved compliance, must be avoided.

Finally it has been observed that despite all the above-mentioned efforts, a prospective study can still be inadequate to collect all the relevant costs and effects, and that models will often be needed to complete the picture, e.g. to predict long-term results. Therefore the final report of a health economic study must clearly show which data come directly from the study and which have been added as input for the model. Reference is made again to section 3.1.1 for further information on prospective health economic evaluations.

---

[63] Ramsey S. et al. Good research practices for cost-effectiveness analysis alongside clinical trials: the ISPOR RCT-CEA Task Force report. Value Health. 2005 Sep-Oct;8(5):521-33.

5 Problems with the interpretation and implementation of health economic evaluations and final considerations

Although the importance of economic evaluations is increasingly recognised in health and healthcare policy, policy makers often appear to have difficulties with the role of these economic evaluations, with the way in which they are carried out and with the way in which the results are interpreted. It is sometimes said that this is due to a lack of expertise and manpower at the policy level. However, it is useful to focus on these matters from the perspective of the policy makers themselves. This reveals the presence of a number of dilemmas. These concern the level of the methodological quality of the studies, the predictive character of the studies and the interpretation and implementation of the results.

With regard to methodological quality, I have already given a summary of guidelines which should allow policy makers and decision makers to judge this quality better. I would like to point out, that despite the existence of these guidelines, health economic studies of inferior quality are still sometimes published. Once again, I argue for the application of design specific guidelines (see previous chapter).

We will now look in more detail at the interpretation and implementation of the results of health economic evaluations.

5.1 When a QALY is not a QALY

Decision making based on health economic studies sometimes appears to produce rather strange decisions, especially at first sight. Stolk et al. (2002)[64] point out that a medicine such as Viagra does not appear to be reimbursed anywhere in the world, despite a better cost-effectiveness than many other interventions. Indeed, Viagra achieves a result of approximately €5,000 per QALY, while a heart transplant costs €47,000 and a lung transplant costs €100,000 per QALY. The latter are mostly reimbursed.

A possible explanation is suggested in an experiment conducted by Eric Nord, a Norwegian health economist, in which he asks a random sample of the general population to make a choice between the funding of 2 therapies.[65] For example, with one therapy a patient (patient X) with a condition of a level of severity 7 can be helped to achieve level 4, on a scale of 1 to 7 (1 = best, 7 = worst). Another patient (patient Y) can improve from 4 to 1 with another therapy. (Note that every step in the scale is of the same size of improvement; that is, the difference between 5 and 4 is the same as the difference between 6 and 5; the difference between 7 and 4 is the same as between 4 and 1). The respondents are told that there is not enough money to finance both therapies and that a choice must be made. In other words: "who would you spend the money on, patient X or patient Y?" Both improve by three levels. The experiment shows that most respondents choose patient X rather than patient Y. Even stronger: the improvement for patient X is on average considered to be 5 times more valuable than the improvement for patient Y. Other comparisons, not necessarily with the same magnitude of improvement (e.g., from 6 to 5, versus from 4 to 2) confirmed that the preference is for *the patient who is in the most serious condition*. In other words, people seem to prioritize the patient who is worse off. This probably explains why treatments for more serious problems are sometimes accepted despite their poor cost-effectiveness, while certain cost-effective treatments are rejected because of an (at least perceived) lower degree of severity.

---

[64] Stolk EA, Brouwer WBF, Busschbach JJV. Rationalising rationing: economic and other considerations in the debate about funding of Viagra. Health Policy 2002;59(1):53-63.

[65] Nord E. The trade off between severity of illness and treatment effect in cost-value analysis of health care. Health Policy 24 (1993) 227-238

However, is the severity of the condition at that moment the only factor, or is more involved? Stolk et al. (2004)[66] introduce the concept *proportional shortfall*. This concept is the ratio between, on the one hand, the number of QALYs that a person would lose as the result of a disease if this disease were not treated, and on the other hand, the normal number of expected QALYs for that person if this disease had not occurred. For example, suppose a person is diagnosed with cancer at the age of 50. If it is not treated, the expected number of remaining QALYs is only 5. But without this disease, the number of expected QALYs would have been 25. The proportional shortfall is then said to be (25-5)/25 = 20/25 = 80%. Indeed, the patient would lose 80% of his potential quality adjusted life years if s/he remains untreated. The authors suggest that policy makers apparently have more money available for every QALY that is gained for the treatment of those diseases with a greater proportional shortfall. Further research is currently being carried out into this concept.

5.2 The impact on the budget

In the previous chapter I gave the example of the cornflakes, in which you do not take the normal course of action and buy the brand with the lowest cost per 100g because it is available only in packets of 100kg and you do not have the budget for it.

The same applies for medicines and technologies: a cost-effective result at the individual patient level may extrapolate to an immense budgetary impact at the population level and this plays a part in the policy decisions. The policy maker will certainly have to take this into account. This can be demonstrated by means of an admittedly abstract choice problem, as presented here below.[67]

Suppose you are the policy maker, and you have a budget of €1 billion available (or, if you prefer, £1 billion or $1 billion). There are seven new possible interventions, as shown in Table 11.

---

[66] Stolk EA, et al. Reconciliation of economic concerns and health policy: illustration of an equity adjustment procedure using proportional shortfall. PharmacoEconomics 2004;22(17):1097-107.
[67] Based on Eddy D. Cost-effectiveness analysis. A conversation with my father. JAMA 1992; 267 (12).

Every intervention has been examined for its cost-effectiveness at the level of the population. We see the number of patients who are eligible, the cost per patient, the total budgetary impact (the multiplication of the number of patients and the cost per patient), the percentage of patients for whom the therapy works, the gain in QALYs for each successfully treated patient, the total number of QALYs and finally the cost-effectiveness ratio.

The sum of the budgetary impact of the seven treatments is €2.15 billion, which is more than twice the available budget of €1 billion. Therefore the policy maker must make choices and set priorities in order to generate the maximum number of QALYs with his limited budget.

5 Problems with the interpretation and implementation of health economic evaluations and final considerations

Table 11. Summary of 7 new interventions in a choice problem with limited budget

	Cost per patient (1)	Number of patients	Budget impact (2)	% success (3)	Gained QALY in case of succes (4)	Total QALYs (5)	ICER (6)
A*	€10000	60000	€600 M	25%	1.4	21000	€28571
B*	€4000	100000	€400 M	2%	9	18000	€22222
C*	€350000	1000	€350 M	90%	19	17100	€20468
D*	€500	500000	€250 M	1%	3.2	16000	€15625
E*	€10000	20000	€200 M	100%	0.6	12000	€16667
F*	€1000	200000	€200 M	50%	0.1	10000	€20000
G*	€500000	300	€150 M	100%	21	6300	€23810

(1) This is the incremental cost of the strategy. For example, A* is a new treatment for Alzheimer's disease and was compared to the current treatment A. The incremental cost per patient is €10,000.
(2) The budget impact is the product of the cost per patient and the number of patients. For A* this is €10000 × 60000 = €600 million.
(3) This is also incremental in relation to the current treatment (see (1)). For instance, with A* the success rate is 85% while this was only 60% with current treatment A → a gain of 25%.
(4) This number only applies for successfully treated patients (in the case of A* this means 25% of 60000 = 15000 successfully treated patients.
(5) This is the product of the number of successfully treated patients and the number of QALYs per successfully treated patient: e.g., for A* this is 60000 × 25% × 1.4 = 15000 × 1.4 = 21000.
(6) This is the ratio between the budget impact and the total number of QALYs, e.g., for A* this is €600M/21000 = €28571.

— 99 —

The solution which results in the most QALYs for the set budget is that in which the interventions are ranked according to the last column, from the lowest (best) to the highest (worst) cost-effectiveness. This is done in Table 12. The interventions that are chosen are those at the top of the resultant list and a line is drawn where the budget is used up). With this solution, 55,100 QALYs are achieved (the sum of the first four lines in the total QALYs column).

This number cannot be improved in any way!

An interesting observation is that the size of the budget (€1 billion) determines the maximum willingness to pay for a QALY (In this example, this maximum willingness to pay is €20,468; see 4th line, right-hand column.)

However, bearing in mind the considerations in the previous section, there are immediate doubts about whether the best choice has been made. It appears that therapy G is not chosen because its cost-effectiveness is not good enough. This is an admittedly expensive but very effective therapy for which only very few patients are eligible. These 300 patients would each gain 21 QALYs with this intervention. Clearly, this is a matter of the possibility of saving the lives of these people, who must be in a serious condition. Will these people simply be dropped while therapy F, which has a moderate success rate and limited gains in QALYs, will be reimbursed? It would not be surprising if policy makers were prepared to reimburse G and not F!

Let us go a step even further and suppose that there is a slight mistake with regard to the starting situation: it turns out that treatment D* does not apply to 500,000 patients but to 1,500,000; and treatment E* applies to 25,000 rather than 20,000 patients. Looking at the table again we find that the budget is used up after only these 2 interventions (Table 13). What policy maker could afford to reimburse only these 2 most cost-effective treatments, and not reimburse the rest? Logically the policy maker will wish to limit the budget impact by putting downward pressure on the price of D*, or reimburse D* only for the highest risk category of patients in order to reduce the number of eligible patients.

This simple example shows the importance of budgetary impact. The problem today is that there is not yet a clear insight into what is thought of as a large budgetary impact and what a small one. This will depend to an important extent on the permitted growth of the budget.

5 Problems with the interpretation and implementation of health economic evaluations and final considerations

Table 12: Solving the choice problem by means of cost-effectiveness

	Cost per patient	Number of patients	Budget impact	% success	Gained QALY in case of succes	Total QALYs	ICER
D*	€500	500000	€250 M	1%	3.2	16000	€15625
E*	€10000	20000	€200 M	100%	0.6	12000	€16667
F*	€1000	200000	€200 M	50%	0.1	10000	€20000
C*	€350000	1000	€350 M	90%	19	17100	€20468
B*	€4000	100000	€400 M	2%	9	18000	€22222
G*	€500000	300	€150 M	100%	21	6300	€23810
A*	€10000	60000	€600 M	25%	1.4	21000	€28571

Table 13: Solving the choice problem with a different budgetary impact for D* and E*.

	Cost per patient	Number of patients	Budget impact	% success	Gained QALY in case of succes	Total QALYs	ICER
D*	€500	1500000	€750 M	1%	3.2	48000	€15625
E*	€10000	25000	€250 M	100%	0.6	15000	€16667
F*	€1000	200000	€200 M	50%	0.1	10000	€20000
C*	€350000	1000	€350 M	90%	19	17100	€20468
B*	€4000	100000	€400 M	2%	9	18000	€22222
G*	€500000	300	€150 M	100%	21	6300	€23810
A*	€10000	60000	€600 M	25%	1.4	21000	€28571

5.3 The need for re-evaluation

Another problem of health economic evaluations is the conclusion that "this is never finished". Certainly when a medicine, or more generally a treatment or intervention is reimbursed, this is on the basis of the data available at that time. For a medicine this is limited to what is known from clinical studies. Hence, in many cases, there are data available on efficacy, but not on effectiveness. Furthermore, a great deal can change after the moment of reimbursement. For example, when activated protein C became available for severe sepsis, health economic evaluations suggested, on the basis of the clinical studies known at the time, that the cost-effectiveness of this medicine was acceptable. A few years later we know better, because on the basis of more recent data it is apparent that the mortality impact is less than what had been expected on the basis of the first clinical studies.[68]

Once a drug is on the market, physicians may also use medication differently from the way in which it should be used according to the studies. Sometimes different doses are used or other indications are treated in which the product may be less cost-effective. Finally there may also be problems occurring with regard to the safety of products, which means of course that everything automatically has to be reviewed.

There are two possible strategies for undertaking a *re-evaluation of cost-effectiveness*.
One is to take an existing decision model and adapt those figures in the model which are known to have changed over time, leading to a new version of the model and a new result. The other is to set up a prospective 'naturalistic' study in which the treatment concerned is studied in real circumstances. The second option is of course a more expensive one, and one should always bear in mind the cost-effectiveness of conducting a cost-effectiveness study!

---

[68] Gardlund B. Activated protein C (Xigris) treatment in sepsis: a drug in trouble. Acta Anaesthesiol Scand. 2006 Sep;50(8):907-10.

5.4 Final considerations

The aim of this book has been to familiarise the non-economic reader who is active in healthcare with the principles and methods of health economic evaluations. The question now is what can be done with the knowledge that has been acquired?

Isn't all this attention to health economic evaluations rather extreme, rather 'over the top'? After all, what physicians do should not be motivated by costs, but by the value of their interventions. Of course, to some extent this viewpoint is right. Nevertheless, it is precisely the extent to which it is possible to gain health for every invested euro or dollar or pound which is the real *value* of treatment. Admittedly, the mistake which is sometimes made is that policy makers look only at costs and forget to take into account the ratio between costs and effects. In other words, what is forgotten is the ultimate goal of health (care) policy, i.e., to produce health. However, the mistake which physicians sometimes make is to consider only effectiveness without wondering whether it is possible to achieve better results in a different way with the same resources.

But how can *value* be measured? The QALY was presented as the 'ultimate' parameter. But there is not yet a great deal of consensus on the way in which these QALY weights or utilities (the score between 0-1) should be measured. There is the EQ-5D approach or the SF36, or the direct way via approaches known as *time trade off* or *standard gamble* (not discussed in this book). Therefore there is a risk of comparing different results which were based on different methods. Obviously it is necessary to guard against this risk and it is the task of health economists to arrive at a consensus in this respect, or at least point out the differences. Eric Nord's example, showing how a QALY can sometimes not be a QALY, poses additional problems to the use of this parameter.

An alternative approach for policy makers is to set priorities in terms of what diseases are most important to treat and then prioritize treatments *within* these disease areas. In this way, cross-disease comparisons become unnecessary and effectiveness can be expressed in disease specific terms.

5 Problems with the interpretation and implementation of health economic evaluations and final considerations

One criticism that is often heard is that the application of health economic principles places the interests of society before those of individuals. For instance, when a decision is made not to reimburse a certain treatment for the metastasis of colorectal cancer because of poor cost-effectiveness, this is to the detriment of an individual patient who could possibly benefit from this treatment. In fact, however, that fact that cost-effectiveness may be moderate for the average patient population does not mean it is moderate for every individual patient. Moreover, the argument of the individual patient - "I have paid contributions all my life, and now that I need an intervention I am not eligible!?" - is justified.

Abrams (1993)[69] offers a possible general solution as follows: "doctors decide what is effective, patients decide what they accept or refuse and society decides what is appropriate". Actually doctors need two 'heads'. One head must think along with policy makers and try to determine what the best decisions are from the point of view of society, on the basis of clinical and health data and given the limited resources. The other must advocate for the patient and aim for his/her maximum benefit within the limitations imposed by society. However, the first head must remain subordinate to the second and only emphasising savings and only serving the payer is in conflict with this principle.

We also must avoid generalisations in health economic evaluations. It is important to look at subtypes of patients in order to fine-tune policy decisions. This also means – in my opinion – that ideally the results of health economic evaluations must play a role in medical guidelines. When these guidelines are only based on clinical information they fail to achieve their goal, i.e. to provide the optimal medical diagnosis and treatment with the resources available. After all, diagnosis and treatment can only be called optimal if their consequences can be paid for by society.

My penultimate consideration (which contrasts with the previous one to some extent) is that, given their inherent uncertainties, it is important to avoid hard claims on the basis of health economic evaluations. It is not so much the final result of the analysis which is most interesting for the decision maker, but rather the dynamics between structure, input variables and result. Sensitivity analyses are actually

---

[69] Abrams FR. The doctor with 2 heads. NEJM 1993; 328 (13): 975-976.

more important than the basecase result because they show us the driving elements in the ultimate relationship between costs and effects.

Finally, we may conclude that health economic evaluations will not *replace* decision making. They are just one element in the decision making process, along with disease severity, budget impact, available treatment alternatives, equity and others.

But I do believe that a decision in healthcare with regard to the optimal spending of resources will be a better and more informed decision when there has been a health economic evaluation than when there has not. I hope that, after reading this book, you will share this opinion.